GHOSTS OF OLD LOUISVILLE

True Stories of Hauntings
in
America's Largest
Victorian Neighborhood

by

David Dominé

International Standard Book Number 0-913383-91-0
Library of Congress Card Catalog Number 2005922415

Cover design and book layout by Asher Graphics

Manufactured in the United States of America

All book order correspondence should be addressed to:

McClanahan Publishing House, Inc.
P.O. Box 100
Kuttawa, KY 42055

270-388-9388
800-544-6959

www.kybooks.com
books@kybooks.com

DEDICATION

For my little buddy, Schnigglefritz,
a little silver schnauzer
with a heart of gold
who left this earth
much too soon on January 23rd, 2004.

As I wrote this book,
he was ever by my side,
providing me with countless nights of solace,
the most faithful of friends till the end,
loyal and true,
keeping the ghosts at bay.

From ghoulies and ghosties
And long-leggedy beasties
And things that go bunp in the night
Good Lord, deliver us!

-Scottish Prayer

TABLE OF CONTENTS

PREFACE

I am not a parapsychologist. I do not even know if I believe in ghosts, spirits, telekinetic energy or whatever else may be the purported cause of perceived supernatural activity. I think people in their melodramatic haste are all too often ready to attribute strange phenomena to would-be paranormal circumstances rather than draw the most logical conclusions. One thing I do know, however, is that individuals do experience unexplained occurrences. Whether or not they can in fact be blamed on mental energy, restless souls, residual views of the past, or just plain imagination is something I don't know, either. Ghost stories, on the other hand, require no explanation and are just that – *stories*. The tales in this book form a collection of stories centered on events and places in the Old Louisville neighborhood in Louisville, Kentucky, a Victorian gem forgotten by time that has seen its share of splendor, sorrow and tragedy. Some of the stories are first-hand accounts of unearthly happenings and others are legends that have taken root in the area. Some of these tales have been documented before, while others make their first appearance in this book.

I am not a historian, either, but rather a curious individual and writer with a penchant for haunted places…and lots of imagination. I make no claims as to the veracity of the information herein. I have done hundreds of hours of research and interviewed scores of people, so these accounts do indeed have a basis in fact; nonetheless, I have exercised a certain amount of artistic license when putting pen to paper. As for the names of the people I spoke with, some have been changed to provide anonymity. When I quote an individual and mention the name, this indicates a first-hand source I interviewed. When I quote other individuals but do not give a name it is because the information is second-hand.

The Old Louisville neighborhood is one of my favorite places on earth, and it is only fitting that it have its share of spooks and phantoms. I am happy to be the first person to compile a written record of the many legends and stories of the supernatural that hail exclusively from the largest Victorian neighborhood in the country. If I have piqued your curiosity and enticed outsiders to come and explore its haunted lanes and alleys, and to discover the charms of its former grandeur, I will have succeeded with this book.

David Dominé
Old Louisville, October 31, 2004

FOREWORD

David Dominé explores paranormal experiences in *Ghosts of Old Louisville*. This pioneering book serves as the first collection of ghost stories I know which unfolds within a familiar neighborhood in the city of my birth. Many of Old Louisville's mansions serve as seminal locations where first events and first experiences unfold in my youth.

Decades later after a performance of my *Murder in Cherokee Park*, Judy Cato introduces me to Mr. Dominé. Dominé and I shake hands on the steps outside of the Clifton Center Theatre in July, 2003. Soon, we three friends form a writers' group. We conduct our monthly meetings in one another's residences.

Like David Dominé himself, his Old Louisville mansion strikes me as exotic, handsome, mysterious, strong, and tall. Intricately jeweled, lacquered, and studded surfaces transport his friends and visitors into extraordinary realms remindful of Byzantine or Russian terems for cloistered royalty.

Dominé's beautifully appointed dining room table overflows with his own gourmet cuisine presented and served with artistic originality; moreover, his writing clearly announces remarkable expertise. He elevates craft into art.

During the winter of 2004, Dominé offers *Ghosts of Old Louisville* for Cato and me to evaluate. The book fascinates because his ghost stories unfold within one of my favorite neighborhoods, Old Louisville.

Mr. Dominé's text merges historical facts and architectural details with an imaginative narrative based upon personal conversations and interviews. Overall, the work emerges as a mood piece, a work of atmosphere.

Mood and atmosphere prove the most difficult aspects of writing for any writer to accomplish well. Dominé's mood and atmosphere convince.

Writers can conceptualize mood and atmosphere from memories. During the 1950s I remember feeling dismay when Urban Renewal demolished several square blocks of downtown Louisville's late 18th and early 19th century brick row houses. Today, I observe their vast stretches of vacant lots, new roads and parking spaces. Only memory can reconstruct those three-story homes' classical fanlights, stone staircases gracefully curving to the sidewalks, hand-blown glass window panes, handsome chimneys, interior moldings skillfully hand-carved by slaves, and thick fire walls.

Obviously, descriptive writing communicates vivid memories of these former structures. Likewise, Dominé's prose communicates former realms and experiences of interesting people living and deceased.

Dominé's spine-tingling accounts of the paranormal recreate a former age. *Ghosts of Old Louisville's* stories occur equally inside extant and non-extant mansions and dwelling places. Also, churches, cemeteries, and a variety of other places appear. Dominé's memories fabricate experiences realized within specific times and places. The fabrications heighten the mysterious.

Mysteriousness in ghost stories is not merely a matter of the writer presenting cobwebs, moans, and shadows for readers. For any subject to appear truly mysterious, some glimpse, however fleeting or miniscule, must convey a sense of the divine.

David Dominé's imaginative agility as a writer illuminates glimpses of the divine. His writing affirms that a glimpse of the divine is possible within everyone, including ghosts from a spirit world.

Like religion, mystery stories focus on the inexplicable. Dominé's ghost stories attempt to explain the mysterious to skeptical readers. His ghost stories attempt to illuminate and to verify miraculous events for doubting readers.

Atheists deny God's existence and believe that everything, including unknowns, is explicable. No atheists can believe in mysteries and ghosts. Obviously, David Dominé's collection of ghost stories proves he is no atheist. He is an artist with words. Additionally, herein, Mr. Dominé is a pioneer with new subject matter concerning his neighborhood.

David's wizardry with vocabulary pleases. Frankly, I enjoy his precision with words. In Dominé's prose, readers don't go up in balloon rides. *How common.* Instead, readers experience balloon *"ascensions."* Dominé daringly utilizes *"albeit."* What other writer today so dares? He creates the comfortable *"enclave"* of a millionaire living in splendor on Saint James Count. The word *"enclave"* suggests a coziness and warmth impossible to achieve in common terms such as "room," "chamber," or "interior."

Dominé's precise placement of modifiers impresses. His writing faithfully reconstitutes exact expression in conversations. *How refreshing!*

Perhaps *Ghosts of Old Louisville* might inspire additional collections of stories pertaining to Louisville. I hope all readers enjoy David Dominé's stories as much as I. I envy readers their first readings of *Ghosts of Old Louisville.* I suggest that readers create a comfortable *enclave* which includes an overstuffed armchair beside a crackling fire in a fireplace. Listen to the late autumn rain pouring in torrents outside the stained glass window. Sip a glass of port. Tuck your legs and feet under a crocheted lap robe. Light a nearby candle. Open Dominé's book. *Could any evening be more enjoyable?*

Jerry Lee Rodgers
Louisville, October 31, 2004

INTRODUCTION

A brisk fall day is the perfect time to stroll the streets of Old Louisville. An overcast sky overhead and dead leaves underfoot - and just enough chill dampness in the air to make you pull your coat tighter around you…this is the best time to amble along the old streets and alleys, admiring the imposing Victorian architecture while the smell of apples and wood smoke spices the air. The boxwood hedges surrounding the mansions and townhouses still have their summer green, but most of the towering trees have lost their leaves and can only rattle bare branches to protest the gathering winds. If you're lucky, you might pass one of the old gas lamps at just the right moment when dusk reluctantly surrenders the last of its daylight to night and hear the click and hiss of the lantern coming on in a feeble attempt to ward off the dark. This is the time that ghosts start to wander the streets of Old Louisville.

It's no wonder that lost spirits should decide to wander one of the most historic neighborhoods in the country. Its streets have seen Victorian elegance and the unbridled opulence of the Gilded Age, the decadence of the Roaring Twenties and the ruin of the Great Depression. And like so many American cities, the lanes and alleyways of its grandest residential area experienced the painful decline and decay of the post-war years before making a gradual comeback to claim its spot as a premier neighborhood. What used to be bordellos and flop houses are now comfortable single-family residences, and it seems that new people – especially out-of-towners – are flooding the area, many of them hoping to find an old home to save.

Generations have lived, loved and died behind these fortress-like doors and no small number of families have made their fortunes here and then experienced financial ruin. How many hearts must have been broken...It's really not surprising, then, that reports of ghostly figures and unexplained phenomena in the palatial homes abound. Even certain corners and church steps are said to have their regular haunts, and strange patches of fog are known to materialize at the base of streetlamps and then spread out over the brick sidewalks before suddenly disappearing.

Old Louisville is a National Preservation District with hundreds and hundreds of structures representing dozens of architectural styles and traditions. In fact, it is the third largest in the nation, covering several square miles, and it is said to be the biggest Victorian preservation district as well. Despite the disasters of Urban Renewal, many blocks have remained virtually unchanged for more than a century, and its homes have borne witness to countless stories and personal tragedy. A walk through the streets of Old Louisville will make you stop and think about these things. When the wind picks up and sets the dead leaves on the sidewalk to swirling, you might wonder who lived – and died – in the large brick mansion in front of you. When the air bristles with the fall chill, you could stop and ask yourself why someone is staring down at you from the third-story window of the large, uninhabited gray stone house across the street or why you hear organ music from the abandoned church on the corner. Take a stroll, and the past comes alive in Old Louisville, especially when the gaslights click on and night falls, and ghosts start to roam the streets.

ABOUT OLD LOUISVILLE

Gargoyles, chameleons, serpents and swans ... turrets, towers, bays and gables ... wrought-iron fences, hand-carved doors, stained-glass windows ... hidden balconies, secluded courtyards, and secret passageways ... terra-cotta, glazed brick, tile, marble and stone ... Old Louisville is a feast for the eyes, and as such, Kentucky can boast one of the most splendid residential neighborhoods in the entire country. A leisurely stroll along the tree-lined streets of Old Louisville can transport a visitor back in time to an era when a man's home truly was his castle.

Victorian Gothic abounds, as do shining examples of Richardsonian Romanesque, Queen Anne, Italianate, Chateauesque and Beaux Arts architecture, making Old Louisville the country's largest Victorian neighborhood. As a National Preservation District, it ranks as the third largest only after Boston and Georgetown. The picturesque boulevards, streets and alleys of Old Louisville boast miles of grand mansions and comfortable dwellings, thousands in all, embellished with architectural styles and elements of centuries past from all corners of the globe.

Old Louisville has a very colorful history – mostly of local importance – and this history is kept alive and well in the many stories and anecdotes swapped in the parlors and salons of its gracious homes. First developed between the 1870s and the early 1900s, many consider the *Southern Extension*, as residents called it, Louisville's first suburb. A major catalyst to its growth came in 1883 when Louisville hosted the extremely successful *Southern Exposition* and received international attention when former resident Thomas Edison showcased his incandescent light bulb. When it finally closed its doors in 1887, savvy developers started to sell off the land on the newly-dubbed Saint James and

Belgravia Courts, realizing that image-conscious Victorians would snatch up anything reminiscent of London aristocracy. The rich and elite poured into the posh "new" neighborhood, and residents applied the name "Old Louisville" to the district in the 1950s.

While "Urban Renewal" caused the destruction of similar neighborhoods all around the country, most of Old Louisville somehow managed to escape the wrecking ball. After a blighted period in the 1940s, '50s and '60s, residents of Kentucky's largest city started to realize that they had a diamond in the rough. Instead of giving in to the planned destruction of priceless examples of architecture, locals banded together and had the entire area placed on the National Register of Historic Places. The Old Louisville Preservation District today includes approximately 48 blocks of the residential core bounded by Kentucky and Bloom Street to the north, and between Sixth Street and Interstate 65 to the east and west.

Old Louisville puts on its finery and southern charm in the springtime, just before the Kentucky Derby in May when crystal blue skies provide the perfect backdrop for a colorful explosion of azalea, dogwood and redbud blossoms. It shines in the crisp fall air of October as well, when hundreds of thousands flock to its quaint streets for the Saint James Art Show and stroll beneath a canopy of spectacular fall colors. Since the 1970s, Old Louisville has undergone an impressive renaissance, but it is still one of the "best-kept secrets" around. About 20,000 people, representing a wide spectrum of ages, incomes, races and lifestyles, make Old Louisville their home today. This diversity, as well as the beautiful, turn-of-the-century Victorian homes and friendly residents, makes Old Louisville an exciting place to live, work and play.

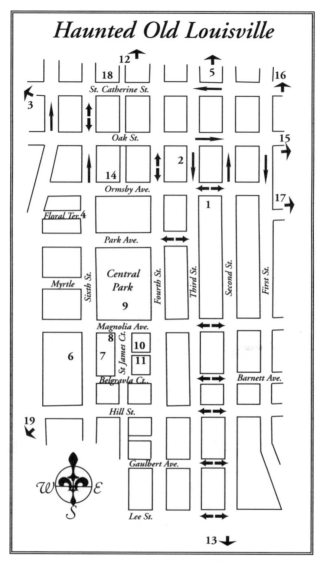

Haunted Old Louisville

1. First Church of Christ, Scientist
2. Widmer House
3. National Tobacco Works
4. Floral Terrace
5. Old Presbyterian Seminary
6. Jennie Casseday's Infirmary
7. The Cabbage Patch
8. Conrad-Caldwell House
9. Old DuPont Square
10. Fountain Court
11. Home of Lady Ross
12. Brennan House
13. J.B. Speed Museum
14. Speed Mansion
15. Brook Street
16. Old Male High School
17. Fort George
18. 539 West Saint Catherine
19. Waverly Hills

Chapter 1

THE FIRST CHURCH OF CHRIST, SCIENTIST

At the corner of Third Street and Ormsby Avenue sits one of Old Louisville's most beloved and visually striking landmarks. Sheathed in white granite and marble that impart a shimmering glow at all hours of the day, it anchors a stretch of Third Street known as "Millionaires Row." An imposing structure originally begun in 1917, the austere exterior of the First Church of Christ, Scientist belies an interior noted for its understated elegance and beauty. Outside, observers see a long porch ensconced by a row of twelve monolithic columns towering along the front entrance, subtly balanced by nine sentinel-like wooden doors topped with mullioned transoms guarding the entrance. Inside, a huge sky-blue clerestory soaring overhead commands attention and lends a sense of airiness to the solid surroundings. Brass torchieres flank several flights of stairs as they drop to the sidewalk below, and locals claim that the spirit of a young woman – also noted for her beauty and elegance – haunts these steps. They call her the *Lady of the Stairs*, and those who have seen her always remark on her singular grace and loveliness.

"She was very statuesque and seemed to be lost in thought, but I noticed right away that she was extremely beautiful. She had ivory white skin, her eyes and hair were jet black, and she was wearing a long, cream-colored gown with lace trim and a ruffled collar like they would have worn around the early 1900s. I saw her, and it literally took my breath away." Donald Spade reports that no woman had ever taken his breath away before his encounter with the *Lady of the Stairs*. A no-nonsense historian employed at the Filson Club Historical Society in the 1980s, his friends describe him as somebody who wouldn't make up stories, either. "If Don says he saw something, then I believe him," says a former co-worker. "He's probably one of the most reliable and trustworthy people I know." Everyone who knew him said the same thing: Don was not the kind of person to make up things.

"I thought I must have been seeing things, since I had just worked fourteen hours straight," he explains, "but the more I stared, the more I realized there was something standing in front of me on the stairs in front of the church. It was a woman, and I wasn't imagining anything at all." It was a cool fall night, and Don had been forced to park across the street from the historical society while workers repaved the parking lot. The spot he found sat directly in front of the stairs leading up to the Christian Scientist Church.

Housed across the street in the former Ferguson residence, a huge beaux-arts mansion built in 1905 and considered by many the largest home in Louisville for its day, the Filson Club has amassed Kentucky's largest collection of genealogical records, local lore and historical documents since its founding in 1884. Reputedly a favorite haunt of neighborhood spirits itself, the sophisticated façade of the structure presents a nice counterbalance to the inherent simplicity of the church's design. For more than fifty years the Pearson family had used it as a funeral parlor, and several workers at the Filson Club had claimed to hear strange noises or feel a strange presence late at night. Don, however, had always dismissed these accounts as the result of overactive imaginations. "Whenever anyone told me they heard steps overhead when no one was there, or that they sensed someone was watching them, I never took it seriously. I didn't think they were lying or anything, but I just didn't think they were looking for a logical explanation when there could have been one. I thought they were a little too eager to blame strange events on ghosts and spirits."

One chilly night in mid-October, however, Don reports that any

The First Church of Christ, Scientist (1917), known for the hauntingly beautiful *Lady of the Stairs* **who haunts its steps.**

skepticism he harbored regarding explanations for other people's strange happenings took quite a beating. Darkness had fallen several hours earlier, and he had decided to leave for home about 9:00 that evening. He turned off the lights in the stately mansion, set the alarm, and locked the door behind him before he dashed across the street to where he had left his car early that morning. The branches rustled uneasily in the trees overhead, and a brisk breeze swept along the sidewalk, scattering dried leaves and adding to the chill in the night air. "It was getting a bit cool, but it was still a nice night, and if I hadn't been so worn out, I'd have taken a walk around the neighborhood, like I very often did. This time I just decided to go home and get some sleep instead."

Stifling a yawn, he unlocked the car door, opened it and slid into the driver's side before putting the keys into the ignition. Enjoying the momentary relief after hours on his feet, he pushed his head back against the seat rest, stretched his legs and listened to the strains of classical music wafting from the radio.

"I started the car and was just about ready to pull away from the curb when I glanced out my window and noticed a strange light on the steps in front of the church. Mesmerized, I put the car in neutral and rolled the window down to get a better look." What he saw sent chills down his spine. Although he knew at an instant that something otherworldly stood before him, he couldn't help but notice how real the vision seemed. "I was looking at a woman from another era; I knew it right away. She looked like a society lady from the turn of the century or something, and it was obvious that she felt out of place."

With the car engine gently humming and filling the interior with a comforting blanket of warm air, Don clutched the steering wheel and stared over his shoulder while the apparition slowly made its way down the flight of granite steps. Her figure bathed in a silvery glow, she had all the trappings of a turn-of-the-century Gibson Girl including the long-sleeved blouse ruffled at the neck and characteristic coiffure. She also wore a long skirt with a wasp waist and a lacy hem that hung over polished, black high-top shoes, however, her feet made no sound as she slowly came down the stairs.

"It was totally quiet and she seemed to float down the steps. But it looked like she had been pacing along the upper stair before she started to come down the stairs, waiting for somebody. There was a far-away look about her and she appeared reluctant to leave the steps. An overwhelming sense of sadness immediately came over me… and then she reached the sidewalk and disappeared, just like that." The whole episode might have lasted ten or fifteen seconds at the most.

"I usually don't use the word *melancholy*, but that's exactly the word that came to mind when I saw her," explains the no-frills historian. "She was overcome with melancholy. I had such an overwhelming sense of sorrow that it made my eyes tear up. And that terrible feeling lasted the whole time I saw her slowly walk down the steps. When she reached the sidewalk and vanished, the feeling of dread I was experiencing vanished as well… just like that!" He sat in the car and stared at the vacant steps for a moment, rubbing his tired eyes and not really sure if he hadn't imagined the whole scenario. Deciding he had indeed witnessed something very strange, he put the car in drive and headed to his condo downtown. After several hours of tossing and turning, he allowed himself to drift off to sleep, but visions of the woman on the stairs plagued his slumber throughout the night.

The next morning he could hardly contain himself at his desk in the Filson Club. "Even though I was opening myself up to ridicule since I had always been so skeptical of other's stories, I went ahead and told a coworker about the apparition from the night before." But instead of ridiculing him, Don's colleague seemed intrigued by the tale. "I had heard one or two stories about the lady on the stairs before, but I had no first-hand experience with her myself," she recalls. "I believe I might even have been witness to a strange sighting in the Ferguson mansion several years prior to that, but I really didn't have much to offer Don, other than an ear to listen with." Although she only lived several blocks down the road and usually walked by the church at least once a day, the middle-aged woman had never noticed anything strange there. Her mother, on the other hand, claimed that she had seen a similar ghost in the 1940s when she was a child, and she had always referred to her as the *Lady on the Steps.*

The elderly woman had unfortunately passed away the year before, so Don decided to try and locate other possible eyewitnesses to the mysterious lady on the stairs. None of his coworkers at the historical society knew much about the supposed haunt, however, and Don found himself with little more than a huge craving to learn more about the woman who haunted the steps in front of the old church.

"For several weeks after that I spent hours rummaging through old documents in the library here, trying to find information about anyone associated with the Christian Science Church or about Old Louisville society in general. I did not find anything at all that might have shed some light on the haunting, but I did uncover a few other stories about ghost sightings in the neighborhood, and this time I wasn't so skeptical when I read them." Although the enthusiasm for his ghostly research gradually subsided, a year later Don still found himself squeezing in at least an hour or two of investigation every week. "I wasn't spending as much time looking for articles and such as I did the first week or two after I saw the spirit, but I was still looking. And to tell the truth, I was sort of miffed that I hadn't found anything to substantiate whatever it was that I had seen. I was starting to think I had imagined the whole thing, but every time I came outside the Filson Club, I couldn't help but stare at those steps in front of the church. When I remem-

22

Ghosts of Old Louisville

bered back to that night, I could recall almost every detail of the vision that night. I know what showed itself on those stairs had to be real."

A week later Don had his first bit of evidence to support his claims that the spirit of a beautiful young woman haunted the steps in front of the First Church of Christ, Scientist on Third Street. Involved in research for a series of articles meant to capture the colorful history and notable characters of Old Louisville, he needed to interview the relative of a neighbor who had worked for local culinary legend Miss Jennie Benedict at her downtown restaurant in the early 1900s.

A student of Fannie Farmer's cooking school in Boston, Jennie Benedict had made a name for herself in the catering business she ran out of the family home on Third Street. After years of satisfying hungry Louisvillians' cravings for her popular beaten biscuits, chicken salad, pulled candy and devil's food cake, *Benedict's* thrived at its final location at 554 Fourth Avenue from 1911 to 1925. Even though the lady herself died in 1928, *Benedictine*, her most endearing creation, lives on in the minds – and mouths – of many in the Bluegrass State to this day. Originally concocted of cucumbers and cream cheese, it served as the filling for her famous tea sandwiches. Today no true-blooded Louisvillian would ever consider hosting even the most meager of get-togethers without the obligatory plate of Benedictine finger sandwiches. With the passage of time, many variations in the original recipe had evolved, and Don now hoped he would get the low-down on Miss Jennie's authentic recipe.

"This lady's daughter lived in one of the large mansions near Central Park, a huge red brick building that had been in the family for many years. I found out that her mother had left behind a collection of original recipes from prominent families in Old Louisville from around the turn of the century, and she offered to let me have a look at them. Her offer included some personal recollections of Louisville's Fourth Avenue during its heyday in the '30s and '40s." After several minutes of waiting, a regal-looking woman in her late fifties answered the door and escorted him to a large salon off the front reception hall.

"After I introduced myself, she apologized for the delay," Don chuckles. "She said they didn't have servants anymore like they used to, so it took her a while to get from one end of the house to another. We sat down in a beautiful corner room with an amazing wood-coffered ceiling and walls covered in green silk. A roaring fire blazed in the focal point of the parlor, a gigantic oak fireplace with a lovely hearth done in very unique blue and green tiles." Noticing his fascination with the fireplace, the lady informed him that the Rookwood Pottery Company in Cincinnati had designed the unusual ceramic tiles especially for the house sometime around 1885 when an eminent Louisville businessman built the mansion for his wife. Looking around at the rich paneling that wainscoted the room and the delicate crystal chandeliers in the double parlor, Don remembers thinking to himself that the gentleman had spared no expense for his wife.

"I didn't get the grand tour or anything, but you could tell that this was definitely one of the grander mansions at the park. It had to have *at least* 12,000 square feet of living space, if that tells you anything." He considered the foyer and paneled grand stairway, with a beautiful curved staircase that gently wound its way up to the third floor, the crowning features. During the day, sunlight poured through art glass windows at various levels and accented the rich woods in dancing tones of green, amber, gold and peach.

Don and the woman talked for a bit about the history of the house she had lived in for the last twenty years, and then gradually got around to talking about her mother's recollections of working with Jennie Benedict. Delighted to find out that the two women actually knew each other as friends and not just employer and employee, he learned that the one lady would help her friend, Jennie, whenever she needed extra help with catering jobs. A half hour passed, and Don soon had more than enough information to finish his research, including substantiation that Jennie Benedict herself insisted on adding a couple drops of green food coloring to give her Benedictine spread its characteristic chartreuse tint.

"I was talking about the Benedictine family residence on Third Street and I realized it had to be near the Christian Science Church, so I decided to ask if this woman – or her mother – had ever heard about the mysterious woman who haunted those steps." The woman paused for a moment, and then smiled before putting her teacup back on the saucer. "She looked at me with some surprise and said 'Oh, you must mean the *Lady of the Stairs*' and then started to tell her story."

Elizabeth, as she now insisted Don call her, had lived most of her life in the same few blocks that surrounded Central Park. Other than a few years in California while her husband brokered tobacco for various markets in Asia and the South Pacific, she boasted that they had never lived anywhere outside of Kentucky. She considered herself a fixture in Old Louisville, and as such knew quite a few stories as well. Apart from the expertise lent her by years of residency in the neighborhood, she felt herself especially qualified to share her own tales of supernatural phenomena and parapsychological experiences since she enjoyed what some called "psychic gifts." Elizabeth had been born with a caul over her face, a layer of membrane that occasionally covers the features of infants who later in life very often develop special clairvoyant powers and paranormal abilities. And although her mother didn't tell her about this until she had started grade school, Elizabeth still knew she had in her ability certain powers that most did not.

For example, she could discern colored energy fields or auras surrounding most individuals and could therefore make judgments about their character and personality. Since Don radiated a pleasantly soft green and yellow aura to her eyes, she believed him to be someone worthy of her confidence. While out in the country on a family outing, a stranger had pointed out this gift to her as a young girl in the '30s. The unknown man turned out to be none other than Edgar Cayce, someone who had already established himself as a pioneer in the field of paranormal studies. A native Kentuckian himself, he had spotted the young Elizabeth while motoring by a field of daisies and brought the car to a sudden halt. Taking note of the golden aura that mirrored the yellow of the daisies, he approached the child and informed her that a great gift had been given to her. To the amazement of her parents, Cayce asked if the girl had been born with a caul.

Her other great skill involved the capacity to see the spirits of deceased individuals. This happened for the first time at age four, shortly after the passing of her grandmother in a tragic accident. Although word of her death had not yet reached the family, Elizabeth announced to her mother that granny had woke her up that morning and wanted everyone to know that she had to leave and would not see them again for a while. When a deputy sheriff showed up later that day with the sad news of the grandmother's death in a car crash in downtown Columbus, no one doubted that the young Elizabeth had the power to see into the next realm.

Her next sighting happened several months after that when her father took her out on a late-afternoon stroll through the neighborhood. Walking by the imposing Church of Christ, Scientist, she observed a shadowy figure in white as it slowly paced along the upper step, seemingly on the lookout for someone or something. When the diaphanous form noted the young girl's gaze upon her, it slowly turned, smiled and then vanished. Somehow, Elizabeth always felt that these spirits were just as aware of her as she was of them.

Don says, "Elizabeth told me that she saw that woman on more than one occasion during her childhood, but the older she got, the fewer sightings she had. I guess that sort of thing is like practically any skill – you lose it if you don't keep in practice. I read somewhere that younger people, especially adolescents, have so much pent-up energy that they make the best mediums and are more receptive to paranormal activity. It stands to reason then that Elizabeth would have seen fewer spirits as she got older," says Don. Although much of her clairvoyance remained, Elizabeth readily admitted that she rarely saw spirits anymore. As for the ghostly female apparition on the stairs, she had little concrete evidence to share. She knew for certain that the lovely young girl still waited for someone who never showed up, and this caused her great pain and anguish. What or who caused her such sorrow, she couldn't say exactly, only that her spirit still pined away on the lonely steps in front of the large church at the corner of Third and Ormsby.

Strangely enough, congregants of the First Church of Christ, Scientist have no knowledge of any ghostly activity in their midst. Nor can anyone recollect any stories or individuals that might tie in with the alleged haunting. All in all, Christian Scientists don't come across as the superstitious or frivolous types, either.

There is, however, someone who for a brief time attended services at this church, and he claims to be every bit a believer in the occult. Charlie Imorde says he experienced a rebellious phase in his twenties when he broke with the family's strong Catholic tradition and dabbled in various other religions, including Christian Scientist. He came from a family of grocers who for decades ran a small store at the northeast corner of Third and Ormsby – directly adjacent to the Christian Scientists – and he frequently found himself sneaking away to listen to readings there. Within a year, however, he had decided that the teachings of Mary Baker Eddy didn't suit his preconceived notions of religion. He quickly moved on to a six-month period when he regularly attended synagogue downtown, however, not before he had an unsettling encounter with the phantom on the steps of the church.

"My uncle was always telling us stories of a strange woman in white he used to see walking up and down those steps late at night, but we all just teased him and told him he was crazy. He was old-world Italian, and very superstitious. Nobody else had ever said anything about a ghost, so we just figured he was a little cuckoo in the caboose." Charlie soon realized he might have judged his uncle too quickly. Late one spring evening he stood on the steps in front of the church, heatedly discussing politics with another young man after their weekly reading group had let out. A warm wind blew softly across the steps, and a cold chill suddenly ran down his spine.

"All of a sudden I stopped talking because I got this creepy feeling," he recalls. "We just stood there, and then out of nowhere this lady came walking towards us. But she wasn't any normal kind of lady, I tell you, she was all white, and you could see right through her!" Charlie and his friend stood transfixed as the shadowy figure in white slowly approached them, and then walked right through them. "It was like she didn't even see us! She just kept coming and walked right through the both of us till she got to the other side of the steps and then just disappeared into thin air. It was truly the creepiest thing I had ever witnessed. And the worst part was, when she passed through us, we turned cold as ice, just as if we were standing in a winter wind."

Needless to say, that ended their argument over politics. The two quickly said their goodbyes, and Charlie ran back across the street to the family shop. "My uncle was restocking the shelves, and I just had to tell him what had happened. When I told him, he just laughed and asked if I still thought he was crazy, and he wouldn't go on until I apologized. He was like that, very proud and stubborn, and I guess I had really offended him. Well, I didn't have any problems with it, so I went ahead and said that I was sorry, and then we talked about what he had seen before." Just as the old man had said on many occasions, he had seen the same apparition of a beautiful young woman on the steps to the Christian Science church, in the evening and usually around 9:30. Charlie looked at his watch. In five minutes it would be 9:30.

"He described the exact same woman that I had seen – to a tee. Hair, eyes, dress…even the way she seemed to float along instead of walk – it all matched what I described to him. The only thing was, he didn't know exactly who the woman was, or any details about her, just that she was waiting for someone. Well, I shouldn't say he didn't know anything about her, because he did have a couple interesting tidbits." According to his uncle, Charlie learned that the young woman had suffered the tragic loss of a young lover, and that she too had died soon after, leaving only her spirit to pace the steps of the old church at the corner of Third and Ormsby. Although the uncle had no first-hand information about the sad love story offer, he claimed to know someone who did, and he promised his young nephew he'd have the old gentleman tell his story the next time he stopped in at the grocery.

Charlie didn't have to wait very long, because the old man just happened to pay a visit the very next day. Charlie recognized him as one of the regulars and had grown used to seeing him all over the neighborhood, but he knew little else of the man, other than his friends used to call him "Red" because of his fiery auburn hair. Even though he had just turned 90, his hair had changed little with age, and despite his years, he still managed to stay active and get around the neighborhood. Charlie's family had a special fondness for the old man since he had worked for them at the counter. Apart from the family itself, Red knew as much as anyone about the grocery business and had been privy to most all of the goings-on in the family store. When the young man realized his uncle had been talking about Red, he quickly approached the old guy and soon had him sharing his own stories about the phantom woman on the church steps.

"Red had worked for my family for at least fifteen or twenty years, and he was real popular with the regulars. And he knew practically everyone in town, it seemed. A lot of people used to stop in just to say hello and have a chat with him, since he was so personable. That's where the mysterious woman comes in, see?" Although he didn't know the young lady's name, Red explained that locals used to call her 'Miss G.' since she was somehow related to the Gathrights up the road. "He wasn't quite sure what her story was, but she was a relative or something and she was staying with them. He had heard that it was because she had a young suitor who didn't meet with her parents' approval, and their way of dealing with it was to ship her off to a relative's." She made it a habit to stop in for a soda late in the evenings, and Red had grown used to – and truth be told, even looked forward to – her visits since she had the reputation for being quite a beauty. People often commented on her stunning jet-black hair, piercing yet demur dark eyes and ivory skin. "The only thing Red mentioned that could be a negative was that she didn't come across as the most-friendly of sorts. Extremely lovely, yes, but not the outgoing type, I guess you'd say."

Given that she had an admirer already, Red conceded to the young man that when he looked back on it all, the young woman probably didn't intend to be unfriendly or anything. "Times were different back then, and respectable young ladies had to act a certain way. If she had acted too nice and friendly, people might have said she was a floozy or something, and this was before the flappers and the Roaring Twenties, so people still had a very strong Victorian upbringing. I think Red was probably interested in her a little, too, and that might have been a way to put a little distance between them on her behalf. Like he said, she already had a boyfriend, so she probably wanted other guys to know she wasn't available."

Even though time had clouded some of his memory, Red could still place the time at 1918 or 1919. The Great War had just ended, and optimism filled the air. Granted, the US had only participated in the last year of WWI, but a sense of national pride and accomplishment pervaded the country nonetheless. Like with most other cities across the land, a patriotic fervor gripped Louisville, and men in uniform seemed to be especially popular. No wonder then, that the young Miss G. had become enamored of a dashing young soldier recently returned from the trenches in the Ardennes. Tall and handsome, observers described him as the perfect complement to the grace and beauty of the young woman he had fallen in love with. The two, it appeared, planned to settle down and marry after a period of courtship that would allow the young gentleman to establish himself and put aside some money for his bride.

Fate, on the other hand, apparently had different plans for the young couple. The young girl's parents had already chosen a husband for her, someone they thought more befitting of her social and economic standing. The son and heir of a wealthy distilling family, the young gentlemen had one semester left at a prestigious university on the East Coast before he would return to Louisville and claim his betrothed. When the young lady's father and mother realized her emotions would not be so easily managed, they sent her away to live with wealthy relatives on Third Street.

Unbeknownst to her parents, the handsome young suitor in uniform had in fact been stationed at nearby Camp Zachary Taylor, and strangely enough, only a couple miles' distance now separated the two lovers. And even though her relatives kept close watch over her, as had been requested by her parents, she hardly considered them tyrants. True, when she called on friends or attended concerts or plays, a chaperon always accompanied her, but they always allowed her an unsupervised evening constitutional stroll up and down "The Street" if she wished. This half hour of liberty she received every night soon evolved into regular rendezvous with her young army suitor.

Red remembers that many people in the neighborhood realized the young socialite used this time to secretly meet her boyfriend, but most felt sorry for her and said nothing about the affair. Some even went so far as to cover for her when her relatives became suspicious and inquired about as to her whereabouts. By all accounts, public opinion sided with the young soldier and the beautiful young woman he hoped to make his bride.

"Red said they used to meet practically every night right across the street where the First Church of Christ, Scientist was being built. They had laid the cornerstone the year before that, and it took them almost ten years to complete it, so there wasn't much there at the time. But they did have the foundations laid, and since it sat on a raised parcel of land, there were some hidden little nooks and crannies where they could sneak away and not be seen, I guess. For several months it went on like that. Red got used to seeing the young woman practically every night he was in the store. She'd come in, order a soda, pay for it, and then leave…"

One night, however, the young woman appeared visibly distressed when she left the store. She returned fifteen or twenty minutes later and asked Red if anyone had entered the grocery looking for her. When he replied that nobody had enquired after her, she lowered her head and made for the street. When Red closed up shop and walked to his own small house a half-mile away, he noticed that she still stood at the top of the stairs. Waiting in the freezing night air as the winter wind whipped about her, she had little more than a black satin shawl to guard against the cold. From her white skin, it appeared that she had already been chilled to the bone.

The next night the very same thing happened. She showed up at her normal time, ordered her soda, and disappeared. A short time later, she returned and asked if someone had been looking for her. By then Red had heard through the grape vine that the two had made plans to elope because the young beauty's parents had discovered their secret meetings. They now planned on shipping their daughter off to stay with relatives in Saint Louis until the wedding they planned for her in the spring. Realizing the inherent difficulty in overcoming a separation of this magnitude, the young couple decided to elope and stay with relatives of his in Chicago while they dealt with her parents' anger and disapproval. He, after all, had very good prospects for the future and came from an upstanding, albeit not wealthy, family. Their plan had been to rendezvous at their usual spot and time, get a ride to the train station and then take a night train to Chicago where they could get married as they wished.

For another several nights, the same scenario played out in the small grocery at the corner of Third and Ormsby. The young lady would come in and purchase her drink, leave, and then return a short time later looking for her beau. She hardly said a word and she appeared highly agitated. The next afternoon as Red restocked shelves in the front of the store, he spotted a young servant girl who worked for one of the families living next to the Gathright house. One of his best sources for neighborhood gossip, he approached her and asked if she had any word about the planned elopement that had generated such a curious buzz among busybodies in the in the back parlors and kitchens along Millionaires Row.

She seemed almost dumbstruck when he asked the question of her. "Haven't you heard?" she stammered, her eyes wide in amazement. "Young Miss G. and her handsome soldier are dead – both of them." The maid became more upset and between sobs revealed that the funerals had been planned for that very day. When Red claimed that to be impossible, since he had seen her just the night before, the servant could only look at him and shake her head in horror. "Oh, no," she sobbed, "they died *five days ago*. Both of them, taken by the flu..."

1918, for those who don't know, saw one of the greatest influenza epidemics in the history of the United States. As the plague-like fever swept across the nation, few cities could withstand the tragedy and human devastation at hand. Louisville, like so many other cities of its size, lost hundreds of inhabitants to the flu. Some four hundred souls succumbed to the illness in the city itself, and at nearby Camp Zachary Taylor over eight hundred enlisted men perished, the handsome young soldier who had courted Miss G. among them. On the night of their planned elopement, he lay overwhelmed by fever on a standard army cot only a couple miles from where his beloved waited dutifully in the freezing night air. Already chilled to the bone and overcome with anguish when she finally returned home several hours later, she too quickly fell victim to the flu and took to her bed. They would both die within three days, neither of them knowing the fate of the other.

Don now feels he has an answer to the mysterious riddle of the Lady of the Stairs. Although he no longer works at the Filson Club, he admits he often finds himself craning his neck in front of the First Church of Christ, Scientist when he travels up Third Street to his new job at the University of Louisville. He figures he must have passed it at least three hundred times in the evening already, and to this day he has yet to have another encounter with Old Louisville's legendary Lady of the Stairs.

ABOUT EDGAR CAYCE

Many Kentuckians don't realize that one of the greatest – and most accurate – psychics the world has ever known came from the Bluegrass State. Known as *the Sleeping Prophet* by many, Edgar Cayce was born on March 18, 1877 near Hopkinsville and died on January 3, 1945 in Virginia Beach, Virginia. Many Old Louisvillians don't know that Cayce spent some time in their midst from 1898-1900 when Old Louisville enjoyed its heyday as the most elegant neighborhood in the city.

An average individual by all accounts, Cayce had the reputation as a loving husband and father, a skilled photographer, a devoted Sunday school teacher, and an avid gardener. Yet, throughout his life, he displayed some of the most remarkable psychic talents of all time. He gave evidence of this budding talent at an early age when, after falling asleep on his spelling assignment, he realized he could master his school lessons by sleeping on his books. Prior to that first experience, spelling had been torture for the young boy; his father was astounded when he awoke and could spell every word in the book perfectly.

In early adulthood Cayce experienced a seemingly incurable loss of voice, and when doctors could find no cause for the condition, the young man entered the same hypnotic sleep that had enabled him to learn his school lessons years before. Through self-diagnosis while under hypnosis, the young Cayce prescribed simple treatment which ultimately restored his voice and amazed the attending physicians.

Others soon discovered that Cayce could do the same for them. He would lie on his back, close his eyes, fold his hands on his chest and, in a trance-like state, answer questions that visitors asked of him. "What are the secrets of the universe?" "How do I get rid of this wart?" "When will I have a baby?" After he helped a well-to-do family cure their sick child in the early 1900s, word started to spread about Cayce's abilities. Soon thereafter the *New York Times* ran an article in September of 1910 claiming "[T]he medical fraternity of the country is taking a lively interest in the strange power said to be possessed by Edgar Cayce of Hopkinsville, Ky., to diagnose difficult diseases while in a semi conscious state, though he has not the slightest knowledge of medicine when awake."

Cayce continued giving these consultations for years, and the responses to the questions asked of him came to be known as "readings." Today many find they contain such worthwhile insights that individuals continue to get useful advice for everything from maintaining a healthful diet to improving personal relationships. From the first psychic reading given in Hopkinsville in 1901 until the last at Virginia Beach, Virginia, in 1944, Edgar Cayce gave some 14,000 clairvoyant readings.

During his life, Cayce demonstrated the extraordinary nature of the human mind day after day. At times, while asleep, he would speak foreign languages that he had never learned – actually holding conversations with those seeking readings. It was even said that this awareness reached across space and allowed him see places he had never been.

Perhaps one of the best-known examples of Cayce's extraordinary powers involves a Louisville pharmacist. The psychic was hundreds of miles from Louisville and had given a *health reading*. As a remedy, he suggested a particular unguent known as *oil of smoke*; however, neither he nor the patient had ever heard of it. When they tried to find it in drug stores, the medicine could not be found. When pressed for more information during another reading, Edgar gave the name and address of the pharmacist in Louisville where the medicine would be found. They contacted the owner of the pharmacy, but the man said he hadn't heard of such a medicine and didn't have any in his shop. Edgar then took yet another reading and – in vivid detail – described a shelf in the pharmacy where a small vial would be found. The pharmacist looked where Cayce had described and found the medicine; it was old stock and had been pushed to the back of the shelf. Today people call *oil of smoke* "beechwood creosote," and it is a common remedy for those who practice holistic medicine or homeopathy.

From information from the Association for Research and Enlightenment in Virginia Beach, VA.

Chapter 2

WIDMER HOUSE

*L*ike many homes of Old Louisville, the unassuming residence at 1228 South Third Street has seen its share of history. Named for its first owners, the Widmer House has stood silently while more than a century's worth of untold events unfolded in front of – and behind – its ornate, Flemish arabesque façade. It sits about halfway between the downtown area and world-renowned Churchill Downs on a small plot of land measuring only thirty feet across and eighty feet deep. As you're leaving down the front walk, if you take a left on Third Street and walk due north for twenty minutes or so, you'll cross Broadway and enter the revitalized downtown entertainment district along Fourth Street. If you take a right and stroll a couple miles due south, you might just hear the starter's bugle at the famed racetrack for the spring and fall meets at Churchill Downs. Either way you chose, you'll see a stretch of antique residential design that experts have called one of the richest architectural experiences in the country, and you'll pass dozens and dozens of beautiful homes, each of them with a story.

Widmer House, for example, saw its first inhabitants around 1895 when it opened its doors for the business manager of the National Tobacco Works. His name was Joseph C. Widmer, and his wife was Kate

Widmer. One of many tobacco houses in a city that produced half of the world's tobacco, the National Tobacco Works employed some five hundred workers and produced more than six million pounds of burly a year. The house Joseph Widmer bought sat on a larger plot of land originally owned by a neighbor to the south, J.S. Bockee, who also worked in Louisville's thriving tobacco industry. Although he had already made a name and fortune for himself as an astute broker of Kentucky's most famous crop, Mr. Bockee realized more money could be made by the sale of land already in short supply at that time. He took his piece of land to the north, removed an older structure there, and then equally divided the plot into two smaller parcels where he built larger homes with identical floor plans.

Rather small compared to other dwellings along Third Street, its roughly four thousand square feet of living space include three floors, six bedrooms, eight fire places, four flights of stairs, one large linen closet and a poltergeist named Lucy.

Although yet to be proven, Charles D. Meyer, Louisville's first and foremost architect of national acclaim, probably designed the spacious town home to make the most of the small plot of land where German, Irish, African-American and Kentucky craftsmen would create a thoroughly modern and efficient home for its time. Erected at a cost of $12,500.00, the house boasts a unique façade that might be more at home in a medieval village in northern Europe or one of the many whimsical movie palaces built across this country in the late 1920s. Or perhaps in a Victorian notion of what a Moroccan-inspired palace in Spain might have looked like. Locals at one time did in fact refer to it as the "Moorish Palace" given its mosque-like finials and dramatic roofline, and it reputedly hosted several lavish parties in the late 1920s that played on the Lawrence-of-Arabia theme.

By this time the Widmers had already sold the house, and ownership had passed through several hands, most of them single females, by the time World War II ended. For most prosperous cities around the nation, the next several decades bore witness to a dark period in terms of urban development, and Louisville, like all the rest, suffered a period marked by neglect of – and flight from – its grandest neighborhoods. Many gracious homes fell victim to the wrecking ball, and mansions in Old Louisville became flophouses and bordellos, passed to absentee landlords or sat abandoned. A look through the *Caron's City Directories* of the mid 1900s shows that a large number of these stately residences served as boarding houses for single men and woman employed in the Louisville workforce.

Widmer house, for example, housed employees of the nearby L & N Railroad for many years, and it continued as a boarding house until the 1970s. Although it had not been totally stripped of its character like other dwellings in the area, the former residence of Joseph and Kate Widmer had seen better days when a small family bought it in the 1980s. Over the next fourteen years – and with no small amount of elbow grease – they patiently converted the former rooming house to a comfortable single-family residence.

Although it had been largely restored on the interior, many people in the neighborhood said it had always looked like a haunted house to them from the outside. The ornate façade had been painted a dingy battle-ship gray that always cast a gloomy pall over it, and a dramatic, steep-pitched gable soared menacingly overhead and warded off would-be visitors like the severe gaze of an unfriendly sentry. A pair of gargoyle-like chameleons bared their teeth and seemed to hiss at passersby from their perches twenty feet off the ground. Time had weathered the terra cotta garland adorning the arched window on the ground floor, and bits of broken stone and brick lying at the base of the house hinted at more damage overhead. Mortar had totally eroded from between the bricks in some spots, and bare tree branches rattled above. The house appeared to be little more than a solid slate of dark gray with numerous cracks and broken sculptural details.

Now the elaborate facade has been restored, repaired and brightly painted. So brightly painted, in fact, that many people in the neighborhood now refer to it as the "Christmas House" because of the abundance of reds, greens and gold leaf. Details practically invisible to prior observers from the street now leap out and dazzle the eyes, and passersby frequently stop dead in their tracks to admire the colorful collection of architectural adornment looming before them. No one today would think that the cheerful house at 1228 South Third Street might be haunted.

That's where I come in. I bought the house in 1999 and have lived here ever since. In keeping with the home's original arabesque charm, I tried to incorporate a Victorian-inspired Moorish motif when redecorating the formal rooms in the house – the front parlor, reception hall and dining room. The small parlor has walls covered in gold anaglypta paper with patterned studs and a ceiling finished to look like gem-crusted Cordovan leather. A gold-leafed panel over the double doors leading into the foyer bears an inscription in Moroccan Arabic that says "Welcome." For the most part, all the changes I've made to the house have met with very positive feedback. Some alterations, on the other hand, did not receive the same approval. That's where the ghost comes in.

When I first looked at the house several years ago, I jokingly asked the homeowner if the premises happened to have a resident spook. Margaret, the owner, had just spent the last fourteen years in the house, and if anyone knew of on-site ghosts or spirits, she'd be the one. "Just one," she answered seriously. "Lucy is her name, and she won't bother you too much...She doesn't like it when you change things around too much, though..." The way she added this last comment as an after-thought made me a bit uneasy; however, the excitement I felt as I summed up the house's potential in my mind quickly erased any misgivings I might have had. Several weeks later, on December 1st, I moved in, and I quickly found myself with much more on my mind than ghosts. A chimney needed to be rebuilt before it collapsed and fell on the neighbor's porch, the roof had three major leaks, chunks of plaster kept falling from the ceiling in the parlor, and a family of possums had moved into the basement. When pictures and prints kept falling from the walls in the kitchen and adjacent butler's pantry, I had no idea that anything other than a poor job of hanging them might have been the culprit. Even after they had been hung the third and forth times – with bigger nails and different locations – most of them refused to stay put.

"Well, did you ask the ghost if it was OK to start hanging things on the wall?" a friend of mine asked as I swept up the broken glass from an 1850s English lithograph of a leviathan pig that hung over the stove. It had just fallen the third and final time. I decided it would look better sitting in the study on an old oak desk that Willie Shumaker used to own. My friend, Wendy, stood with her hands on her hips and stared at me while some other people went to admire the newly decorated 12-foot tree that stood in the front parlor. "Well, did you?" she demanded. "A house this old has got to have a ghost. My grandmother had a ghost in her house and she always said when you moved into a new place you needed to ask the spirits there if it was OK. Or else they'd cause trouble for you…"

I had totally forgotten Margaret's comments about the resident ghost not liking things changed around too much in the house. I rolled my eyes and scoffed at her as I took the dustpan and walked to the trash-can to deposit the last bits of broken glass I had collected. Just then, a loud crash echoed through the bottom floor and sent a deafening thud reverberating through the walls. Afraid yet another fully loaded Christmas tree had toppled over onto the hardwood floor, we both ran to the front of the house with teeth clenched to survey the damage and destruction. The small group of friends gathered in the parlor had run into the foyer and awaited us with the same expectant look of dread, heads turning on crooked necks to see through the dining room and dis-cover what had fallen *in the kitchen.* We all exchanged puzzled looks and wandered from room to room searching for the source of the loud com-motion. From the sound of it, we all decided that a large chandelier must have fallen somewhere. In the parlor, the tree stood stock still, anchored in place by an invisible bit of wire that stretched between the crown molding and the top of the trunk.

A thorough search of the ground floor yielded absolutely noth-ing and then moved to the second and third floors as well with the same result. We pulled down the steps to the attic and searched it to no avail and then made our way back down through the house and ended up in the basement. Nothing there seemed to explain the loud noise and shat-tering glass we had heard either, even though I had spied a pair of beady possum eyes glowing red in a dark corner. A quick run around the out-side of the house in the frigid winter air resulted in the same puzzled looks and lack of explanation.

Back in the foyer, Wendy assumed the same hands-on-hips posi-tion and glared. "See?" she crowed. "You have to OK it with the ghosts first!" Before I could shrug it off with another scoff, she went to the counter and picked up the hammer lying there and began waving it in the air. Punctuating her words with it as she spoke, the hammer had been raised over her head and waved to and fro. *"If you won't do it, I will!"* Trying to look as imploring and respectful as a mad woman wildly waving a hammer about could, she raised her eyes and shouted. "Dear Ghost Person, we just want to hang some nice pictures back here! You'll like them, so please don't knock them down anymore. We don't want to bother you and we understand it's your house. *Thank you!*" I flinched at the last comment, and Wendy started gathering nails so she could make better use of her hammer. Within five minutes she had managed to rehang all but one of the pictures that had fallen. The pig lithograph would still go to the study, but it needed to be reframed first.

A week later it proudly sat atop the old oak desk in the study, and in the kitchen all the pictures had managed to stay where Wendy had hung them. Back in the kitchen, she had assumed her usual stance and slowly turned around to admire her handiwork, a smug grin painted on her face. "See? I *told* you so..." She emptied her glass of Ravenswood Zinfandel in one gulp and opened another bottle. Once again, the same group of friends had gathered for our usual Thursday-night dinner, a weekly tradition we've managed to keep alive for the last seven years or so. Even though I had been in the house only a couple of weeks, it already had a cozy, homey feel to it, and we sat down in the dining room for a dinner of Bibb lettuce salad with smoked trout, roasted pork tenderloin, mashed potatoes and red cabbage. By the time we passed around generous helpings of bourbon gingerbread and whipped cream for dessert, little mention had been made of the ghost.

"So, what did the previous owner tell you about the spook in the attic?" Tim inquired in a nasally tone as he sloshed generous amounts of Woodford Reserve in large snifters before passing them out to those assembled around the dinner table. Fondly named "Skippy" by his closest friends, Tim worked at Brown Forman's Labrot & Graham Distillery in Versailles, one of the first distillers in the state where they produced the small-batch Woodford Reserve bourbon. We took our whiskey and moved to the fire in the front parlor while I repeated Margaret's warnings that Lucy didn't like to see things changed around too much. *"See? I told you so..."* Wendy cackled.

"Maybe we should get out the *Ouija* board and see if we can contact her..." suggested Skippy, looking around the room for approval. "Ay, no, mama mía, no..." Ramón stood up hastily and bolted for the kitchen. "No way! I don't like those things. They're *bad news!*" He had disappeared and left behind only a trailing epithet of curses in Spanish.

In the kitchen something glass suddenly crashed to the floor and broke into pieces, causing us all to jump. We stared at each other and waited. *"Ramón?* Was that you...*or the ghost?"* Beth, a lawyer friend who had showed up just in time for dessert, stood up and sat her snifter on the lovely art nouveau mahogany mantel. Ramón showed up at the parlor doors with a meek smile on his face. "Oops..." He held up a small piece of broken glass. "I broke one of your Waterford champagne flutes... *Sorry."*

An hour later we had finished our drinks, and I closed the door as the last of the guests headed out into the wintry night air. I tidied up a bit, made the rounds of the rooms to turn off the lights and jumped into bed. Only after I had snuggled in under the warm covers with Rocky and Bess, my two miniature schnauzers, did I recall seeing that the pig print on the desk in the study had fallen or been turned over so it lay face down. I debated getting out of bed and standing it up again, but another sudden loud noise downstairs startled me, and I got out of bed to investigate that instead, Rocky and Bess trailing cautiously behind. It seemed to come from the small bathroom under the main stairs on the first floor, and the closer I got to it, the more it sounded like a hissing noise. Pushing the door all the way open, I turned on the light, and inside I could see the little black cat we had recently adopted. She stood on all fours with her back arched and hissed at something unseen. Then she ran into the tiny closet next to the toilet and refused to come out. This had become her new home as of late. Ever since we had moved into the new house, the previously mischievous troublemaker had turned into a literal *scaredy cat.* No amount of coaxing would make her leave the confines of the tiny bathroom, and she wouldn't even eat or drink unless someone brought her food and water. After several minutes of reassuring pats, I left her to the little closet and returned to my bedroom on the second floor, deliberately ignoring the chandelier that slowly swung back and forth in the hallway at the top of the servant's stairs. When the strong smell of coffee awoke me the next morning, I had all but forgotten about the disturbance with the cat and the swinging light fixture.

Christmas came, and it seemed that the house would burst with a steady stream of family, friends and out-of-town visitors that didn't abate until holiday decorations came down on the sixth of January. The dreary weather that followed in the next two months provided ample opportunity for our small group of friends to meet in front of the warm fire in the front parlor, and it seemed that I had effortlessly transplanted myself in a cozy home that felt like a familiar friend. I looked forward to the warmer weather of spring just around the corner, not only for the pleasant temperatures, but also for the chance to do some major work around the house. Three rooms sat totally empty, in need of furniture, wallpaper and drapes, and I couldn't wait to tear up the outdated shag carpeting that covered the entire second floor and redo the hardwood underneath. The crumbling façade would have to wait until the following year, and in the meantime I would occupy myself with details like repairing plaster walls and searching antique shops for period-authentic light fixtures and furnishings. I still had to get rid of the possums in the basement, but that could wait. After all, they must have been cold as well.

When April finally arrived, it seemed as if spring had come overnight, and the neighborhood just as quickly transformed itself into a fresh garden of new greenery and branches of all sorts, heavily laden with buds ready to erupt in an explosion of verdant splendor. By the end of the month and the start of the annual Kentucky Derby festival, the early tendrils of summer had already taken hold, and the humidity and warmth in the air hinted at the many sultry summer evenings that lay ahead. Azalea bushes danced with hundreds of animated blossoms in scarlet, crimson and fuchsia, and dogwood branches displayed delicate petals of pink and ivory at every turn. And tender sprigs of mint seemed to shoot up wherever a neglected patch of moist soil would permit – around the gas lamps on Saint James Court, where the wrought-iron legs of old benches dug into the damp earth of Central Park, at foundations and through the cracks in cobblestone and brick courtyards.

For most people in Louisville, fresh mint in April usually means that the annual Kentucky Derby is right around the corner and that mint juleps are in store. People pull out rare silver cups and cocktail shakers, long-necked spoons passed down from one generation to the next, and secret family recipes…all in anticipation of the one time of the year even the strictest of teetotalers will allow themselves this one indulgence. It seems that the two weeks before the actual races can barely contain all the parties, and at no time of year do the southern drawls sound as marked as they do in the time leading up to the Derby. From the grandest mansions to the most humble cottages, debates rage as to which bourbon makes the best julep, if indeed one should use crushed or shaved ice in the drink, and whether the tender sprigs of mint should remain in the cup after they have been bruised with a silver spoon to release their fragrant oils.

I had just returned from one of these parties the Sunday afternoon before the Derby when I found myself in the kitchen at the back of the house. Puzzled once again by the strong smell of coffee that pervaded the room, I suddenly felt a chill run down my spine at the realization that no one had made coffee the entire day. As a matter of fact, no one had been in the house since I left that morning around 11:00. The lone chill erupted in a rash of goose flesh when it occurred to me that I had been totally alone the several times prior to that when the curious coffee aroma had awakened me in the morning. I moved next to the stove, and it seemed that the smell intensified and I could almost feel the warmth of coffee brewing on a front burner. Although I had employed several men to redo the hardwood floors on the second story a couple of days before that, they would not be back until the following Tuesday, and they had the only spare key to the house. I looked in the sink for any evidence of coffee making and found none. When the phone started ringing I ran to the front of the house to answer it.

A high-school friend was calling from Texas and she was eager to hear more about the new house. An archeologist, she couldn't get enough when I told her a bit about the layout of the house and the historic neighborhood. "Do you have any ghosts?" she inquired when I told her I had discovered a 1907 inspection sheet from the Louisville Electric Company in an old-fashioned fuse cabinet on the second floor. I chuckled and told her about the pictures falling, the strange noises when I first moved in and the several times I had come across the unexplained smell of freshly brewed coffee, and I carefully added that I considered myself a skeptic. She listened as I recounted some of the details, and I suddenly caught my breath when I heard a door on the third floor slam shut. "What?" she demanded, obviously somewhat alarmed. In a hushed tone, I told her to be quiet for a second as I listened to the footsteps that started down the stairs. "I think there's someone in the house," I whispered. The telephone stood on a small table under the main stairs, and I stretched the cord to position myself to see up into the stairwell, but all I saw was darkness. Tread by tread, I could distinctly hear footsteps as they slowly made their way down the stairs, from the top floor, to the landing and then the second floor.

"Someone is coming down the stairs!" I told her, waiting as the steps continued down from the second floor to the landing just a few feet away from where I stood. *"I can hear footsteps,"* I added. The stairs from first floor to the second floor doubled back midway at the landing, obscuring it from sight, and I expected someone to appear at any moment. It sounded like the invisible steps had reached the last landing and a pair of feet would materialize as they rounded the bend and came down the final section of stairs. I held my breath and waited, but the steps simply stopped, the unknown source concealed in the shadows. I had the impression that someone had just walked all the way down the stairs and stopped on the very last step necessary for her to stay out of view.

I set the phone down and flipped on the light in the stairway. "Tell me what's going on there!" insisted a tense voice from the other end of the line. "Are you OK?" I had already run up and down the stairs and found no one by the time I picked up the phone and gave an update. I had seen nothing at all, and I had no idea at all where the sound of feet coming down the stairs could have originated. I shrugged my shoulders and said it must have been the sound of wood expanding and contracting due to the warmer weather, perhaps aided by the sanding the workers had given the floor. "Hmmm…maybe your ghost doesn't like what you're doing to the house," volunteered my friend. My blood ran cold as I remembered the warning I had received about the temperamental Lucy.

I chuckled a nervous laugh and then mentioned that she hadn't been the first one to think of that. We spoke a couple more minutes, and then I said good night and hung up the phone, careful to leave the light on in the stairwell. I walked into the kitchen and set the teakettle on the stove, relieved to notice that the strong smell of coffee had dissipated. However, whatever sense of uneasiness I had experienced quickly returned when I realized the temperature in the room had dropped to almost freezing. I checked the thermostat, and although it registered 65 degrees, it seemed that an icy wind had filled the small space. Pushing any negative thoughts out of my head, I waited for the water to boil, made my tea and ran up to the study on the second floor. After doing a bit of work on the computer, I watched a movie, and when the pot of tea ran out, I decided to turn in for the evening. I ran downstairs to set the teapot in the sink and then called the dogs to go outside. My dog Bess, a kind and nurturing soul, had become enamored of the possum, and she refused to budge from her post outside the closed door to the basement till I nudged her with my foot and forced her along.

The back door propped open, I watched them run around the back yard a bit and then called them inside. Before I had the chance to close the door all the way, a black blur shot past me with a sharp hiss, ran out the door and disappeared over the back fence. The nervous little black cat had abandoned its home under the stairs and refused to return home, something it had never done before. She had never even been outside, for all I knew, so I got in the car and drove around the neighborhood looking for her. After half an hour and no luck, I decided to return home and resume the search the next morning if she hadn't come back by then. Once inside, I turned off the lights, gathered the dogs, and then we all headed for bed.

Even though spring had definitely arrived, it seemed that a bit of a chill still remained in the house, so I settled in under the covers and quickly drifted off to sleep. I had slept for perhaps an hour or so when the uneasy stirring of the dogs on the bed roused me from my slumber. Despite the darkness, a small patch of light from the street illuminated the bed through the window, and I could see both dogs as they stood and looked towards the hallway, a low growl barely audible as Rocky lowered his head and stared. I pulled them both towards me and calmed them down, then listened. At first I could hear nothing, but then I heard a long, slow, wooden creak. I thought maybe a door had swung open by itself, and I waited to hear more. A minute or so passed, and I heard nothing, so I lay back down and waited to fall back asleep. Once again, a long, drawn-out creak resonated slowly in the hallway and sent chills down my spine. I thought someone had surely broken into the house, and I attempted to visualize his location in relation to my bedroom.

Another moment passed, and I heard another long groan from the floorboards in the hall, this time closer to the bedroom door in front of me. I could see both dogs as they cocked their heads in response to noise, and I suddenly realized I was afraid. Almost paralyzed, I listened as something seemed to make its way up and down the hallway that ran from the large study at the front of the house, past the home's original nursery, my bedroom, the linen closet and bathroom to the small bedroom in the rear of the building. After several minutes' hesitation, I finally mustered the courage to hurl all 220 pounds of me out of bed, grab the *Louisville Slugger* propped against the wall and switch on the light. Making as much noise as possible, I rushed out of the room to confront the unseen intruder, the bat wielded overhead as I cautiously ran the length of the corridor and turned on several other lights. Finding nothing, I searched the other two floors and even looked around the attic and basement before returning my bedroom.

I closed the door this time, and once tucked under the covers again, I tried to convince myself that I hadn't gone crazy and had just imagined the sounds of an intruder in the hallway. After several minutes, I started to relax, comforted by the thought that the closed door would offer some sort of protection in the unlikely event I started to hear the strange noises again. Even if they did start up again, I'd be fine, I told myself, as long as the weird noises did not bother me *inside* the bedroom. Another minute or two passed, and a loud groan from the floorboards echoed from the left side of the bed, just *inches* from where I lay. My skin started to crawl at the realization that the noises had not only returned, but had *entered* the room. Fighting the sense of panic welling up inside me, I forced myself to take slow breaths and reassured myself all would be fine, as long as the noise stayed on the left side of the bed. Several tense moments of silence dragged on, and I dreaded the idea that the strange creaking would move around the bed to my right-hand side. Suddenly, the floor let out a long, moaning squeak that ended with a loud pop, and my eyes involuntarily squeezed themselves shut. The creepy, wooden groan had come from a spot at the foot of the bed. Despite the warm breeze drifting in through a small window next to the bed, a cold chill ran down my spine and set my heart to racing even faster. I kept telling myself it had to be the result of the wood expanding and contracting due to the warmer weather, but if it moved all the way around to the right side, I decided, I would be leaving.

I held my breath and waited. The dogs seemed to be holding their breaths as well. One minute passed, and then another, the lengthy silence compounding the tension that hung in the darkness. Another minute went by, and I slowly exhaled as quietly as possible. I listened intently and squinted to better discern any movement in the darkness, all the while overcome with the uncomfortable sensation that someone or something was watching me. Bess lowered her head and slowly stretched out on the bed, and I cautiously relaxed a bit, my ears still straining to hear the slightest noise. I turned my head to the right and struggled to make out any shapes in the blackness, but I still saw nothing. Then, the same long, drawn-out type of creak reverberated through the floorboards *next to the right side of the bed,* as if an invisible visitor had taken a step or shifted his weight while standing there. The loud noise faded into a soft echo, and then I heard what sounded like a pluck and strum on the strings of a harp.

I literally flew out of bed, grabbed my cell phone and baseball bat, and – making sure the dogs were behind me – ran down the stairs as I pulled on my bathrobe. The door slamming shut behind us, we ran out the back way and piled into the car. The clock on the cell phone read 3:30 AM, and after turning the key in the ignition, I dialed a friend's number to let him know I would be coming over. I looked back at the house, almost expecting to see the windows all aglow with an eerie red in the darkness, and when I saw nothing, I started to reconsider the decision to leave. My friends would certainly never let me forget it. Before the phone started to ring on the other end, I hung up and decided to go back...in a bit. There had to be a perfectly logical explanation for the strange happenings. Rocky and Bess reluctantly got out of the car and followed me back to the house.

Once inside, I closed the door and listened intently. Total silence reigned. Not completely convinced that I had imagined everything, we sat down in the small room between the kitchen and dining room and watched TV until the sun came up around 6:30. Stifling a yawn, I trudged back up the stairs to the bedroom on the second floor and managed several hours' sleep, content at the fact that I was able to unwind for the first time in over seven hours. After I woke up, I took the dogs for a short walk and then decided to run some errands. As I gathered my keys and wallet in the kitchen, I noticed the strong smell of freshly brewed coffee again. Two workmen had arrived and could be heard working on the floors above me, so I walked up to them and inquired if either of them had made coffee or maybe brought any along. When they both answered in the negative, adding that they never drank coffee, I did my best to ignore the uneasy feeling that overcame me, but a slight shudder still ran the length of my spine. Still hopeful that something logical would explain the weird noises from the night before, I also asked if the sanding and warmer weather might account for an increase in the creaks and groans that had pervaded the house in the last couple days. One of them shrugged his shoulders and said "It happens, I guess," but his coworker just gave him a skeptical look. "I never heard it happen before," he finally decided. Not reassured either way, I left the house to do my errands.

Later that afternoon I returned home, eager to check the progress that had been made on the hardwood floors. Although an entire week had passed since the work started, most of the time had been spent pulling up the old carpeting and removing nails and staples imbedded in the boards. Curious to see if they had managed to sand more than just the front room they had begun several days prior to that, I walked into the house and followed the loud drone of a drum sander upstairs. The scent of fresh pine and sawdust permeated the air, and I made a room-to-room inspection while waiting for the noise to stop. Pleased with the progress that had been made, I walked up behind them when they finally turned the sander off and said hello. Both of them literally jumped out of their skin at the greeting. "Lord, you scared me to death!" the older of the two said with a sigh. He looked at his companion and chuckled uneasily. "Were you in the house before, about an hour or so ago?" the other inquired. I told them that I had just arrived home minutes earlier and asked why. "We were positive someone was in the house." Both men looked down the hall towards the small room that sat at the back of the house. "They kept slamming the door shut back there." I assured them that I had not been in the house since they had last seen me and asked if they had seen anyone. The younger man scratched his head and scowled a bit. "No, but we sure got the feeling somebody was watching us."

I walked back to the room and stuck my head through the door. A small, plain room that sat directly above the kitchen, the workers had decided to save it for last. When they finished the three rooms at the front of the house, they would work their way down the hallway and then start to pull up the carpeting in this, the final room. I looked around and saw nothing out of the ordinary, save for a thick layer of dust that had settled on the mantel and the dressing table, despite the sheets of plastic hung over the doorways to contain the fine sawdust stirred up by the sanders. I noticed a thin layer of dust in the hall leading up to the room I had just entered, but other than my own two footprints, nothing hinted at a possible explanation for the slamming door. I closed the door and turned to go downstairs, but before I moved from the spot I heard what sounded like three knocks coming from the other side. Startled, I quickly opened the door and peered inside, not at all surprised to see nothing in the room. I walked to a window and looked out into the back yard, but nothing showed itself. Then I noticed what seemed to be the smell of a hot iron and freshly pressed laundry, although something about the odor didn't strike me as quite right. It had that starchy, burnt smell an iron gets at a very high setting when it threatens to burn delicate fabric and when build-up starts to collect on the bottom. Thoroughly unnerved, I left the room and ran downstairs, unable to shake the feeling that a pair of invisible eyes followed me.

Despite my trepidation, the next couple of days passed without event, except for various loud creaks and groans easily attributed to normal sound effects in an old house during warm weather. Several mornings I also happened to wake up to the pleasant aroma of fresh coffee downstairs, however I assumed a generous breeze had carried it on from a neighbor's kitchen. By the time Thursday rolled around, I had already attended ten different Derby parties, and with several days to go till the actual *Run for the Roses,* I found myself looking forward to a little quiet time. That would have to wait, though, because I had my own party to attend to, and guests had already started to arrive, many of them regulars from our weekly get-togethers.

Many of them had already heard about the strange sounds that had driven me from the house on the weekend, so talk naturally tended to gravitate towards Lucy and any part she might have played in the matter. "Maybe she was a guest here once and she starved to death, so she's come back to haunt you…" volunteered Gregory from alongside the dining room table. He looked down at several empty silver trays and dabbed a moistened finger in the remaining crumbs. A loud cackle echoed from the doorway to the kitchen, and David, another close friend, emerged with a large platter heaped with hors d'oeuvres from which he replenished the depleted trays. "I'll make sure I don't starve," he quipped. Not content with the small cocktail plates on the table, he ran back to the kitchen and returned with a large dinner plate stacked high with Benedictine finger sandwiches, beaten biscuits with country ham, chicken salad and smoked spoonfish. On a second dinner plate he had artfully arranged a large assortment of candied pecans, bourbon balls and miniature chess tartlets for his own personalized dessert selection. With a shrill laugh, he informed us he didn't want to be disturbed and walked into the parlor to eat.

"If you do have a ghost," someone said, "it was probably someone who used to live here. That's the way is usually works." I had already done quite a bit of research about the house, including a retrieval of all the prior deeds to the property, and nowhere had I come across the name Lucy among the previous female owners and inhabitants. I shared this bit of information with my friends as I passed around a tray of *Modjeska* caramels.

"Well, maybe one of the previous owners had a visitor or a family member who died here in the house," someone offered, popping one of the local treats into her mouth. "Even if no one died here, chances are, they had the body laid out for the wake or funeral. That's what they used to do in the olden days." I helped myself to one of the candies as well, enjoying the sweet rush of marshmallow and caramel that filled my mouth.

"Yeah…back then, they had dead people lying around all over the place. Thank goodness we've got funeral parlors nowadays." David had walked back into the dining room and fixed himself another mint julep. He grabbed the three *Modjeskas* remaining on the tray and walked back to the front parlor. "Someone's at the door," he yelled back over his shoulder. I ran to the door and let in another group of people, and before long talk had shifted to the incredible spring weather and the upcoming races. After another mint julep, Lucy was all but forgotten.

That would soon change, however. The next few nights I hardly got any rest at all since loud footsteps, creaks and groans had kept me from sleeping. Friday night was so bad that I called two friends and asked them to come and spend the night. Of course, when they arrived at 3:30 in the morning, the loud knocks at the back door that kept waking me up and the eerie moans in the back room had all but stopped. Although I hesitated at first, afraid they might think I had lost my mind, I told them the most frightening part had been after I had run down to the back door the third and final time. I had heard three distinct raps and had run to see who was at the back door. Each time I got there, the last time just seconds after hearing the knocks, I could see no one. I was climbing the back stairs when all of a sudden the curtains on the window in the stairwell billowed out in front of me, as if blown by gale-force winds. I became all the more unnerved when I remembered that the window had been sealed shut and painted over. Not so much as the tiniest draft of air could be felt when I examined it later. My friends just looked at me and shook their heads. "Uh…you really need to do something…and soon."

The Derby came and went, leaving in its wake a spell of hot weather that brought locals out to their front porches to enjoy the sultry evenings that have made Old Louisville summers famous. By the time the next week rolled around, people were glad to be done with parties and looked forward to a return to the mundane. When I awoke Thursday morning to the overpowering smell of hot coffee in the kitchen, I was actually happy that I had no plans for the entire week. I wanted to be there when the men arrived to work on the hardwood floors upstairs, but other than that, I had nothing that had to be done. I planned on being away from home as much as possible until I figured out what to do about the strange happenings at Widmer House.

"Whew! That sure is strong today!" commented one of the workers as they walked through the back door into the kitchen. He wrinkled his nose and looked around the room. "Did you ever figure out where the smell is coming from?" I responded that I thought it must be coming from the neighbor's house as the two made their way up the back stairs. "We'll start on the last room today and should be done in another day or two," commented the older of the two men.

They headed upstairs to do their work, and I left to do some errands at the bank and the post office. When I returned late that afternoon, the strong coffee smell in the kitchen had faded, only to be replaced by the familiar smell of a hot iron and fresh laundry. I scratched my head and looked around, then walked into the next room. Upstairs, I could hear a loud scraping noise, the irritating sound of wood against wood. It appeared to come from the linen closet on the second floor, and from the loud footsteps running back and forth, it sounded like the workers had decided to concentrate on that room instead of the small room at the back of the house. I couldn't figure out exactly what they were doing, however. It sounded like they were pulling out the huge wooden drawers for sheets and pillows, and then pushing them back in again. *In, out, in, out...* The incessant scraping noise had really started to annoy me.

I was just about to run up the back stairs and demand an explanation when the back door opened, and in walked the two workers. "*What...?*" I looked at them with a stupefied look of disbelief and then bolted upstairs to the linen closet. Although the cupboard doors remained open, and the large storage bins and drawers pulled all the way out, no sound could be heard, except the two workmen as they trudged up the steps behind me.

"Let me guess..." the older gentleman said as he reached the top of the back stairs, "you heard all kinds of racket in this linen closet here, like someone was running around and pulling out those big wooden bins there."

"Yes," I answered, "but how..."

Before I had a chance to continue, the younger man cut me off. "Man, this place is *haunted!* That's all there is to it. We kept hearing strange noises the whole time we were here, and it felt like someone was watching us, too." He looked at the other man.

"*Yep.* We took our lunch break an hour ago because we couldn't stand it anymore and didn't want to be here alone. This here door kept slamming shut, too." He pointed at a door outside the linen closet that divided the long hallway on the second floor into two sections of equal length when it was closed. Although I had heard it slam shut many times, I assumed it had been the result of the breeze from an opened window.

"And come take a look at this," he said as he motioned for me to follow him to the small room at the back of the house. "Remember that iron smell you were always complaining about?" The room had been stripped of its outdated carpeting, exposing the beautiful century-old heart-of-pine flooring underneath. He stopped in front of the fireplace and pointed to a spot on the floor. Although the wood had lost much of its original luster due to years of neglect and build up, I could easily make out the dark shape he pointed to. It was about five inches long, and triangular, but the two longest sides were slightly rounded. A shudder ran down my spine as I realized I was staring at a burn mark on the floor left behind by an old-fashioned *flat iron*…

I ran back to the dividing door in the middle of the hallway, and as I stood and stared at it, things slowly started to make sense. I closed it, and realized it divided the front half of the house from the back half. The front half included the original lady's day room I now used as a study, the former nursery and another bedroom, all of which had interconnecting doors and doors that opened onto the front part of the hall. From the hall, one could mount the carved oak stairs to three bedrooms on the third floor, or take them down to the public rooms of the house – the parlor, foyer, dining room and small bathroom under the stairs.

I explained this all to my group of Thursday night friends when they arrived for our weekly dinner half an hour later. Opening the door, I ushered them through to the *back* half of the house and then closed it again. We stood in the dark rear corridor and studied the layout in silence. Doors granted entry to the large linen closet, several smaller closets, a bathroom and water closet, and the small bedroom at the very back of the house. The plain back stairs lead down one flight to a small coat room and the cellar stairs, and then into the butler's pantry and the kitchen at the back of the residence. For the most part, all the strange activity had centered around the back part of the home.

"Oh, I see!" exclaimed my friend Laura. "The back part would have been where the *servants* worked and had access. Our heads slowly turned to the small room where at one time a hot flat iron had charred its mark on the floor. "*That* must have been the maid's or the housekeeper's room."

"Do you think *Lucy* could have been a former servant here?"

We all walked back downstairs and debated the possibilities over tall glasses of *tobacco baron's punch*, a potent concoction of bourbon, gin, sherry, lemon juice, and grenadine that Skippy had just discovered while doing research at the distillery. Laura had volunteered for cooking detail, and around the table we soon passed rolls fresh from the oven and a large tray of grilled asparagus with a shallot and bourbon vinaigrette. After that, we sat for hours and enjoyed delicious roast chicken, corn pudding

Circa 1895, Widmer House is reputed to be the home of a mischievous poltergeist named Lucy.

and scalloped potatoes with garlic and tangy cheese from a local Trappist monastery.

Before devouring a dessert of homemade paw-paw ice cream and freshly baked butter cookies, we all knew what had to be done. Walking from room to room in the servants' area of the house, we all followed Wendy as she reassured Lucy that she was free to enjoy the house as she

When workers uncovered this burn mark left by an old iron, much of the strange activity at Widmer House ceased.

wanted. No one wanted to bother her, Wendy said, and we understood that she was just keeping watch over *her* part of the house. We drank coffee and talked till the wee hours of the morning, and other than laughter and lively chatter in the front parlor, not a sound was heard that night at Widmer House.

Since then, not much out of the ordinary has happened in this old house. I finally captured the family of fat possums in the basement and set them free out in the country when the weather warmed up. And none too soon, either. Bess had discovered a gap in the heating grate from the basement to the kitchen and learned that she could drop her doggie treats through it to her possum friends below. Our little black cat, unfortunately, never did return to her little closet under the stairs. I'm sure someone in the neighborhood took her in. That's how people are around here.

Most of the rooms have been completed, and little by little, the house on Third Street is regaining much of its former splendor. Each time I attempt a major project, however, I make sure to clear it with Lucy. Once in a while, something strange might happen, like at Christmas time when the stockings over the mantle in Lucy's room tend to disappear and then reappear in different parts of the house, but for the most part, I get the impression Lucy is content with the current arrangements.

Several months after the last big episode I had an unexpected visit from an elderly lady who said her grandmother had been one of the first owners of the house. She asked to come in and see the place, and I was more than happy to oblige her. As I showed her from room to room and listed to her comments about what changes had taken place and how she approved of the decorating, I grew anxious to hear her comments when we reached Lucy's room at the back of the house. Sure enough, she confirmed that the housekeeper had indeed lived in that room, but other than that, she couldn't recall anything in particular about this person.

When I asked if the name *Lucy* rang a bell, she shook her head and said she couldn't recall any Lucy who had lived in the house. One thing she did remember, she informed me, was that her grandmother's housekeeper had come to her as a young girl, and that even though she was very fond of the girl, she always complained about her mischievousness. With a chuckle, the old woman told how her grandmother was constantly scolding the girl for eavesdropping when she had visitors in the house. Instead of staying out of sight in the back part of the mansion as servants always did, the young girl liked to sneak to the front staircase and listen to conversation in the parlor, making sure she stayed just out of sight in case someone exited the parlor and spotted her in her perch on the stairs.

I thought about the times I had heard footsteps on those stairs and wondered if the mischievous young housekeeper had wanted to eavesdrop and nothing more. Each time I had the distinct impression that someone was trying very hard to stay out of sight. For now I have to content myself with speculation. But – little by little – Widmer House does give up it secrets. I will be patient and some day hope to find more clues about the identity of the real Lucy, if that indeed was her name.

ABOUT THE
NATIONAL TOBACCO WORKS

When Joseph Widmer used to take his private carriage to the corner of 18th and Main every day in the 1890s, the National Tobacco Works was a major hub of activity in a thriving part of the city. While the iron strain and screech of railroad cars echoed in the background, the clip-clop of hooves on cobblestone punctuated the air as workhorses pulled wagons loaded down with burley tobacco. Businessmen in dapper three-piece suits and brokers with waxed mustaches cut deals while newly-arrived immigrants and second-generation freed men of color toiled in the humid confines of the warehouses. On the streets, men yelled and cursed in a variety of tongues and accents ranging from German to Irish brogue.

Today, however, time has virtually forgotten this part of the city. Just minutes from the grand avenues of the city's first suburb, the former main building of the National Tobacco Works sits abandoned and practically in ruins. Once one of the most important tobacco houses in the nation, today broken windows and weathered brick can only hint at the structure's original appearance. The imposing building at 1800 West Main Street is only a ghost of its former self.

Not surprisingly, some residents of this historic West-end neighborhood believe that ghosts still roam the decaying interior of the National Tobacco Works. Strange lights have been seen passing from window to window, although locals claim they see them in parts of the building where the floorboards have rotted through to the next story. On some nights a shadowy figure can be seen darting around the sides of the brick structure, but when police come to investigate, they can find nothing. It could be nothing more than vandals, but then again, individuals have spotted disembodied spirits in the form of apparitions on other occasions.

"It was just after dark, and I saw this black man walking across the floor in front of me," says Rick Harris, a former city planner who had a strange encounter on the second floor of the tobacco factory while there to assess the condition of the property in the 1980s. "He was wearing old-fashioned britches and a dirty, white shirt like a blouse, and it looked like he was carrying a bale of tobacco or something. He also was wearing an old-time cap on his head and looked just as real as you or me. Then he just faded, and I couldn't see him anymore."

Harris, like others, says he could almost hear the sounds of a bygone century in the background as well – wagons with creaking wheels pulled by work horses, the slamming of heavy sliding doors on railroad cars, men toiling and sweating to earn their wages, voices whispering from the past...

The National Tobacco Works today.

Chapter 3

FLORAL TERRACE

During the heyday of Louisville's grand Southern Exposition in the 1880s, the area that now comprises Old Louisville also attracted large numbers of visitors to its immensely popular botanical gardens. The Dumesnil family flower beds, known for many years as the *Floral Gardens*, sat just catty-corner to Central Park near the northwest corner of Sixth Street and Weissinger Avenue (Park Avenue after 1888). During the warm-weather months, people flocked in droves to the cool shade of those gardens and wandered among the rows and rows of rare ornamental shrubs and flowers on display. The area would later become *Floral Terrace*, one of Old Louisville's famed *walking courts* designed to replace the noise and bustle of street traffic with a private splash of green that gave residents a park-like setting in their own front yards.

One of many hidden oases tucked away within the confines of Old Louisville, Floral Terrace has secluded, charming gardens and quaint homes that haven't been discovered by many area residents themselves. On the west side of Sixth Street, about halfway down the block between Park and Ormsby, a small brass plaque in the sidewalk marks the entrance to the tranquil court. If you happen to stroll down the narrow brick pathway that cuts its way down the middle of the tidy row of neat houses facing each other and then cross the alley, it seems that the small front yards suddenly explode in a brilliant green shower of shrubbery, grasses and flowers. At the center, a small fountain splashes peacefully, and if you sit at one of the little wrought iron benches and pause for a minute, you realize that you hear only the cool splash of water and the pleasant rustling of leaves in a soft breeze. Sometimes, as you're sitting there lost in thought, a fellow interloper might wander by and remark with a pleased sigh that she "had no idea this lovely space even existed." Such is the nature of Floral Terrace.

Some residents of this quaint neighborhood, however, believe that the idyllic gardens and tidy facades of Floral Terrace hide a more sinister history. According to local rumor, a large tree that once stood in the center of the court served at one time as a *hanging tree* for various lynchings in the 1800s. The charming little fountain now occupies this site, and late at night, residents have reported sad moans and sobs coming from that area, and some even claim to have seen the disembodied ghost of a man swinging from the end of a rope in mid-air.

"It looked to be a black man, from what I could tell," says Homer Waite of an eerie apparition he claims materialized before him as he sat at the fountain one summer evening. "I was just sitting there, enjoying the warm summer night all by my lonesome," the lifelong resident of Old Louisville recalls, "when this thing just started to take shape in front of my eyes. In a minute or two it was clear enough to recognize, and I was able to see it was a hung man hanging from a rope. *And he was still swinging back and forth, ever so slightly.*" Homer claims the scene reminded him of a lynching, although the only lynchings he ever saw happened on television or in photographs in the newspapers. "Well, I'm not one to get scared off too easylike," says the septuagenarian, "but I decided right then and there it was time to get off my *keester* and find some place else to sit myself down. So I left."

Homer says he had heard plenty of odd stories about his neighborhood, but never had he heard ghost stories concerning a lynching tree on Floral Terrace. "No one ever told me nothing about a hanging tree on that path when I was growing up," he explains. "But after I saw that thing swinging from the rope that one night, I started asking around, and sure enough, quite a few people started saying that they had always heard there was a tree used for lynchings there at one time." Homer claims an uncle told him that an unfortunate black man had been left hanging there for days in the 1870s after a mob unceremoniously executed him for looking "improperly" at a white woman. No records can be found to substantiate these claims; however, as Homer explains, "it was real easy to cover up stuff like that way back when."

According to many historians, Louisville – to a large extent – was spared the lynchings and mob violence so typical of other larger cities in the South; however, some feel it would be quite a stretch to assert that outsiders viewed Louisville as an overly tolerant locale as regards racial issues in the late 1800s and early 1900s. Compared to other cities in the southern states, Louisville stood at the forefront in many issues of racial importance; nonetheless, unfortunately large numbers of the population adhered to the institutionalized forms of discrimination based on ignorance and hate that frequently cast a pall on the southern landscape of the first postbellum century. Although Kentucky itself bore shameful witness to many lynchings from the 1860s through the 1920s, many seem to hold the notion that Louisville managed to escape the sight of these atrocities.

In his excellent book *Life Behind a Veil: Blacks in Louisville, Kentucky 1865-1930* George C. Wright explores the complex history of black/white relations in the Derby City, attesting that "Louisville was spared the lynchings of other cities in the deep south." His thorough record of individual social injustices and police violence nonetheless points an accusing finger at a society rife with ignorance and intolerance that could have easily bred a culture of vigilantism.

Wright relates a well-known incident, for example, from the late 1880s involving the only black player on the Toledo baseball team when they played in Louisville. Moses Fleet Wood Walker had tried to play once in Louisville before that, but the team manager caved in to public uproar and benched him when Louisville fans protested the presence of a "negro" on their all white-pitch. The second time Toledo played at Louisville, the manager stood his ground, however, and allowed Walker to play. Despite his normal talent on the field, Walker gave a dismal performance due to the constant barrage of boos, hisses, and derogatory comments during the game. The enraged home fans had reportedly gone so far as to hurl various items from their perches in the stand at the lone

Do the quiet gardens of Floral Terrace hide an old Louisville secret?

black player in their midst.

Wright also makes mention of the notorious Lieutenant Kinnarny, a rogue policeman known for his "unconventional" ways of dealing with blacks in late 19th-century Louisville. Kinnarny, it seems, had an unfortunate penchant for shooting at innocent blacks who happened to be running away from him. When asked why he did this, he usually replied that "they were acting suspicious." In his book, Wright makes it painfully clear that black Kentuckians of the late 1800s and early 1900s enjoyed very little security in Louisville.

Is it any wonder, then, that across the country, angry mobs of ignorant and misguided souls routinely "strung up" innocent individuals of color? Although extremely hard to find documented accounts of lynchings in Louisville and its surroundings, it is not entirely implausible that legends of lynchings have some actual basis in fact. Given that some local authorities often supported vigilantes, covered up their actions or even participated in the crimes themselves, no one can really say with certainty that a lynch mob *never* in fact paid a visit to the huge wild cherry tree that used to stand at the center of Floral Terrace.

"I looked for hangings and such in the Louisville papers from the time after the Civil War to the early 1900s, and I never came across any accounts of lynchings," says Roscoe Tuttle, a native of Louisville whose family owned a home in the Floral Terrace neighborhood for many years. "I did read articles about lynch mobs and what they did in other parts of the state, but I couldn't find any about Louisville." Despite his lack of success finding reports to substantiate the rumors of lynchings, Roscoe claims he believes local lore nonetheless. "Both of my granddaddies told me they personally knew of a hanging there in the late 1800s, so that's good enough for me, I guess."

Not only that, but Roscoe had an "experience" in the 1970s that he claims made him realize the area had a sinister past. "What I saw made a believer out of me," he explains. "It was so awful a sight to behold that something terrible like a lynching must have produced it." Like other individuals in the quiet neighborhood surrounding Floral Terrace, Roscoe Tuttle believes he saw the apparition of an unfortunate man who died there in the late 1800s.

"You have got to understand that I come from a family where spooks and spirits ain't anything out of the ordinary," he explains. "Part of my family is city people and the other part is country folk, that I'll grant you, but we all was raised believing in ghosts and haints and that spirits from another place was all normal and fine." Although he never used the word, it seems that Roscoe's family had quite a few *superstitions*. "My granny said never to give bananas to a baby, or else it would die, so we didn't. They also said not to be out running around after dark, or else the gypsies would get us and take us away. I figure now, it wasn't always right, what they told us, but when you're young you believe your elders."

For this reason, the young Roscoe always tried to stay away from the center of Floral Terrace after dark. "They told us we'd be found dead the next day if the dead man from the hanging tree got us. So we always stayed away from there."

Little did Roscoe Tuttle imagine that he would get a visit from the dead man from the hanging tree years after he had matured and grown out of the family superstitions. "I still lived in the family house," he explains, "but both my parents had long since passed. And my grand-parents had all been dead for ages." Roscoe lived around the corner from Floral Terrace in a small shotgun house on Park Street, and although he was just steps from the quiet gardens and neat homes of the terrace, he didn't venture out from his house as much as he used to.

"One night I decided to go out for a stroll because it was such a nice night out, and I ended up at the center of Floral Terrace," he explains. "The air was nice and warm, and I was just standing there, looking at the houses and how they had been fixing things up, when all of I sudden I could hear this loud creaking sound." In the dark he couldn't see where the sound came from, but he stood there for five or ten minutes, listening to the rhythmic sound of creaking wood. "The sound never stopped. I'd hear a loud creak and then a softer creak, a loud one, then a soft one, and it just went on like that for what seemed like forever," he says. "At first I thought it was a big tree branch knocking about in the wind, but when I really paid attention, I noticed that there wasn't so much as the slightest breeze that night."

"I was just about ready to give up and walk back to my house," Tuttle recalls, "when I noticed something out of the ordinary in the air in front of me." The elderly gentleman claims that the figure of a man materialized in front of him, suspended in midair with a rope around his neck. "He looked like he was dead, like they had just hanged him, and I couldn't believe my eyes. I knew he had to be *the dead man from the hanging tree* people used to talk about!" Frozen in place, Roscoe could do little more than stare while the scene before him etched itself in his memory.

"It was a black man, I think, and it was just an awful sight, with his head off to the side at an unnatural angle," says Roscoe Tuttle. "His eyes were all bugged out, and I realized that the weird creaking I was hearing matched up with his swinging back and forth. I couldn't see an actual tree branch or anything, but that must have been it. It sounded like a tree branch creaking under his weight as his body swung back and forth." Roscoe says he had seen enough and returned home.

"I was really spooked," he admits, "even though I grew up hearing about stuff like that. I only half believed it and never thought I'd actually see something some day. I didn't know what to do. What do you do in a case like this?" After a couple hours in front of the television, Roscoe had relaxed enough to retire for the evening, and he went to bed. He didn't get much sleep, though.

"I had fallen asleep and must have been that way for two or three

On Floral Terrace, a calming fountain now occupies the alleged site of a large tree once used for lynchings. Some locals believe that restless and tortured spirits still wander the neighborhood in search of justice.

hours," he remembers. "I suddenly opened my eyes and was wide awake for some reason, though. I was just laying there on my back, staring at the ceiling, when I realized I was not alone in the bedroom." Roscoe saw something standing to the side of his bed that sent chills down his spine. As his eyes focused on the dark figure standing there, he realized it was the man he had seen earlier that evening. "He was just standing there, not moving at all, like he was watching me or something. Unlike when I had seen him before, he was alive this time, not dead!"

Although he admits to feeling terrified, Roscoe claims that he didn't feel threatened by the strange figure at his bedside. "I had the feeling he wanted something, that's all. Maybe he wanted us to know they had lynched him and he was innocent or something," he says. "A lot of the black men who were lynched back in the olden days were innocent, isn't that so?"

Roscoe Tuttle thinks about two minutes passed before he closed his eyes and "willed" the ghostly figure to leave. When he opened his eyes several seconds later, the dark figure had vanished, much to his relief. "When something like that happens, you start to second guess yourself," he confesses. "I had to stop and think whether or not I hadn't been dreaming or hallucinating. Just like with the hanging ghost I had seen earlier that night, it seemed so real as I was seeing it, but then afterwards, when it had disappeared, it seemed that it couldn't have happened." Mr. Tuttle says he got up and made himself a cup of hot milk with honey, and a half hour later he drifted off to sleep again.

However, that would not be the last of his encounters with the dead man from the hanging tree of Floral Terrace. Several nights later while brushing his teeth in the bathroom, he received another unanticipated visit from the dead man of the hanging tree. This encounter left him even more "spooked" than the first two. "I had just had my supper and was brushing my teeth over the bathroom sink," he recalls. "The sun had just gone down, and I planned on watching a little television before I hit the sack."

He finished brushing his teeth, rinsed out the toothbrush and then put it back in the medicine cabinet over the sink, not prepared for the sight that awaited him when he closed the door and saw his reflection in the mirrored front. "It was just like in one of them horror movies," he recalls, "because someone else was standing right behind me in the mirror! It was the black man from the hanging tree, only this time he was a lot closer than the other times. He was standing right behind me and I could see his entire face, with those red, bloodshot eyes bugging out at me!" Roscoe says he gasped and then spun around, but he found nothing whatsoever behind him in the bathroom. "When I looked back in the mirror, he was gone, too!"

Tuttle claims the restless soul returned to haunt him several nights after that, each time appearing by the side of his bed, or caught in brief glances in the various mirrors around the house. "Finally, I couldn't take it anymore," he says. "I went and saw a friend who lives nearby and who used to be a Presbyterian minister. He studied at the old seminary down on Broadway way back when, and he always used to talk about ghosts and stuff. So I asked if he could help me." The ex-clergyman came the next day, and the two men walked together to Floral Terrace and sat till the sun went down. Tuttle says his friend lit a candle and then said a short prayer designed to release an earthbound spirit. After another five minutes passed, they returned to his house on Park and had several cups of coffee. Roscoe Tuttle says he received no more visits from the dead man on the hanging tree after that.

Perhaps someone will find documentation someday to substantiate claims that a tree that once stood at the center of Floral Terrace served as lynching tree, but for now, neighborhood residents will have to content themselves with local legend and lore. And it seems that legend abounds on Floral Terrace. In 1933, a May 9 article from the *Your Street and Mine* column of the *Neighborhood Reporter* picked up on these legends of a killing tree. One report has it that that a distraught black man shot himself there after losing his life's savings at nearby Churchill Downs. As a reminder against the evils of gambling, residents supposedly buried the body where they found it – just steps from the infamous hanging tree of Floral Terrace.

ABOUT THE OLD PRESBYTERIAN THEOLOGICAL SEMINARY

Around the turn of the last century when local craftsmen started gathering the immense blocks of Bowling Green white stone to build the Presbyterian Theological Seminary at 109 East Broadway in downtown Louisville, Broadway had a much different appearance than it has today. It compared to the grand thoroughfares of large cities in this country and Europe, and boasted dozens of impressive public buildings, houses of worship and handsome mansions. A couple of blocks down the street, another recent addition, the Norton Hall of the Southern Baptist Theological Seminary had just joined the streetscape in 1895. Next to it, the towering steeple of the Warren Memorial Presbyterian Church had soared over one of the city's busiest streets since the 1870s. Together, they made one of the most spectacular sights to behold along Broadway, a gothic concoction of arches, stained glass, lacy spires, Flemish dormers and spindled turrets reaching heavenward.

Today, a used car lot occupies the site, and large stretches of Broadway have become eyesores for the local population. William Dodd, however, would be happy to know the stone masterpiece he designed over a hundred years ago escaped the fate of so many of the other buildings that once graced Broadway. Today, the old seminary, or Barret Hall as it was known, still sits near the corner of Second and Broadway, but the campus of Jefferson Community College has slowly surrounded it, and it now serves as the Jefferson Building. Every day, hundreds of students walk through the spacious courtyard and into the front lobby, most of them not knowing – or caring – about the history of the stately, gothic structure. Most of them, however, have heard about the ghost of Barret Hall.

Louisville Magazine and local newspapers report that a ghost has been so active that the chief of security keeps a file documenting all the strange goings-on in the century-old building. Unseen hands have turned doorknobs. People frequently hear footsteps when nobody is about, and the elevator goes up and down on its own, carrying seemingly invisible passengers. Lights flicker and go out for no apparent reason, and employees have even reported a shadowy figure in the halls that dis-

Allegedly one of the most haunted locations in the city, the Old Presbyterian Theological Seminary adds a nostalgic touch of Victorian Gothic to the Louisville cityscape along Broadway.

appears when they get close to it. The ghost has even been known to leave mysterious letters in different parts of the building. The spook supposedly scared two employees so badly that they quit their jobs.

In 2000, when I taught Spanish and German for Jefferson Community College in the old seminary building, I heard many stories from fellow employees who had alleged supernatural experiences. One former security guard, Wendell Coates, claims he had an odd encounter while working late one night, making the rounds and checking that the doors and windows had been locked. About 3 o'clock a.m. he found himself in the former library and stopped to sit and rest for several minutes before he continued on with the routine inspection. Nothing out of the ordinary had happened, but as he sat there, he noticed a cold draft sweep through the room. His hair stood on end, and he suddenly came to the realization that a presence had entered the room. Suddenly, his flashlight dimmed and went out, even though he had just put new batteries in the day before. Sitting in the dark, he says he saw a misty figure in white appear and walk slowly over to the fireplace before vanishing. "I wasn't sure, but I think it was a lady. I don't get the feeling she wanted to hurt anyone."

Many of the students and staff at Jefferson Community College think the ghost could be that of Lucy Stites Barret, the wife of the man who had the structure built so many years ago. An inscription in her memory can be read over the fireplace in the area that used to be the library, and word has it that James Rankin Barret had it inscribed as a sign of devotion to his beloved wife. Over the years, several mysterious notes have been found in her favorite parts of the building, and every Halloween it seems that someone coincidentally – and unexpectedly – finds a letter or scrap of paper announcing the presence of Lucy Stites Barret. A freshman on her way to chemistry found the most recent note in the chapel last year. Bearing the initials "LSB," it read: "I am with you alway."

Chapter 4

JENNIE CASSEDAY'S FREE INFIRMARY FOR WOMEN

he house at 1412 South Sixth Street doesn't fit in with the rest of the houses in Old Louisville. While the vast majority of neighborhood homes are of brick construction set back on a small plot of land, this one is not. Sheltered beneath the leafy shade of towering oak trees, it sits back from the street behind an ancient wrought-iron fence, far removed from the everyday activity of Old Louisville as the days silently pass by. Strangely out of place, but nonetheless grand and imposing, it has whitewashed trim and weathered gray clapboard shingles that might seem more at home in a quaint seaside village in New England. In all of Old Louisville, not a single building bears the slightest resemblance to it. Almost in its shadows, a smaller outbuilding in the same style sits next to it and a little further back. If you pause and study the two buildings from the sidewalk, you get the distinct impression that something more than just architectural style alone makes them unique. Dark and foreboding, 1412 South Sixth Street has a secret to tell.

Unlike other stories in this book, I had to hunt down the secret of 1412 South Sixth Street. In most cases, people came to me with their stories, or referred me to other witnesses of paranormal activity in the

Plans for the Jennie Casseday Free Infirmary for Women, named for one of Old Louisville's most remarkable philanthropists, were drawn up in 1892 as a tribute to the still-living woman.

neighborhood. I interviewed the various individuals and then did research to see if any corroborating evidence could be found to verify the substance of the stories before compiling them and putting pen to paper. In the case of 1412 South Sixth Street, I started with the assumption that a story would pop up somewhere along the line, and I set out to see what I could find. Although it required a lot of time and patience, I was not disappointed.

My first line of investigation involved the usual poking around to see if people in the neighborhood had heard anything or knew anything useful about 1412 South Sixth Street. When told the street number alone, most had no idea which building I meant, however, when I added a description of the weathered shingles and mansard roof covered in gray slate, all set behind two stone gate posts, they knew at once which house I inquired about. Although no one knew anything in particular about the house, they all came to the same conclusion: If there wasn't a story there, there ought to be, because 1412 South Sixth Street looked like a haunted house.

Next, I did a title search to learn something about the past owners of the property. Unsuccessful every time I had knocked at the door in hopes of finding someone to talk to in person, I decided to uncover the year of construction and see what I could dig up regarding previous residents. Due to problems at the courthouse and mistakes made when recording the titles, this proved to be a time-consuming endeavor as well, so I decided to do what I usually do in cases such as this: Wait and hope that something would show up.

And that's precisely what happened several months later as I found myself rummaging through books about Louisville history at the Free Public Library. I returned to scan the shelves in a section I usually patronize and managed to come across a book that had somehow escaped my attention before: Clyde F. Crews' *Spirited City: Essays in Louisville History.* I grabbed it from its perch and began perusing the pages, making notes here and there when I found any useful information. Several minutes later I found myself staring at an old black-and-white picture that captured my attention on page 21. It showed an elegant Old Louisville residence, or so I thought, with several younger women standing in the spacious front yard, all of them in starched, white Victorian dresses with high, ruffled collars. It looked oddly familiar, but for some reason, I couldn't place the building and thought it must have been one of the unfortunate many to fall victim to the wrecker's ball. Below the picture, the caption read: "(1895 photo) Jennie Casseday's Free Infirmary for Women." I stared at the large building shingled in wood again, and then it dawned on me. This was an early picture of 1412 South Sixth Street!

Eagerly, I read on and learned what little I could about this early Old Louisville hospital and its founder, Miss Jennie Casseday. It seems that at one time quite a few hospitals dotted the city of Louisville in general, and Old Louisville in particular, a fact attributed to its unenviable geographic position along the somewhat stagnant waters of the Ohio River Valley. As the author explained on page 17, "As the young town matured into its second generation, disease became the greatest stalker of human life. Abetted by the area's large amount of swampland, epidemics decimated the area, providing Louisville's earliest and least desirable nickname: *The Graveyard of the West.*"

In addition to the problems with tuberculosis and cholera, Louisville had to deal with the normal big-city health problems associated with poverty and poor sanitation as well. Like most American cities of the late 1800s, Louisville had started to recognize the plight of the poor in its midst, and one of the main concerns became the deplorable conditions for those living in the city's slums and tenements. The Cabbage Patch Settlement House, a house of refuge and aid for many of Louisville's poor in the early 1900s, still exists today, just steps from the elegant mansions and graceful homes along tree-lined Saint James Court. Although first founded in 1910, the Cabbage Patch relocated in 1929 to a part of Old Louisville still considered the outskirts of the neighborhood, a section of the district where comfortable two and three-story homes start giving way to more modest bungalows and shotgun structures before completely disappearing a couple blocks over on Seventh Street.

When friends of Jennie Casseday built her Free Infirmary for Women in the late 1800s, right across the street from today's Cabbage Patch Settlement House, the area still had pigs running around in fenced-in yards, and even scores of fowl and the occasional cow. Recognizing the added burdens of pregnancy and child care placed on many women of the lower class, Jennie Casseday hoped to provide free health care to the women who needed it most. Casseday, a devout Methodist and member of the Holiness Movement, also saw it as her Christian and human duty to help those less-fortunate members of her community. When associates planned the state-of-the-art facility in the

1890s they saw Casseday as a sort of champion for the rights of the down-trodden, and especially the everyday working girl. Not surprising, unwed mothers, worn-out housewives of the lower class and abandoned women of all ages comprised the majority of her clientele. With this knowledge in hand, I knew there had to be a story somewhere. All I had to do was find it.

A year passed, and I had found almost nothing, something that I regarded as incredibly irksome. I discovered that it had at one time been called McMurtry's Infirmary, but that took me to dead ends as well. An old-timer from the neighbourhood informed me that the slate used on its roof had come originally from the main pavilion of the Southern Exposition, the largest wooden building in the world at the time, when it ended in 1887. I had also hunted down several prior inhabitants of the building after it ceased its functions as hospital and clinic, but no one had experienced anything unusual on the premises or had heard of any-one else who had. The closest I got was a chance encounter with an elderly gentleman at the Saint James Art Show whose father had been born at Casseday's Clinic, as he called it, in 1898. His father had died long since, and the gentleman lived in Louisiana now, so he couldn't offer much more than a few recollections and a heavy southern drawl. I got my break a couple weeks later when I got an insatiable urge for a double latte made with half and half as I was walking my two schnauzers down Belgravia Court.

A new coffee house had just opened up at the corner of Fourth and Hill Streets, and as Rocky and Bess led me through the east gate and out onto Fourth Street, I realized some coffee would hit the spot. I don't really care for the coffee at the Old Louisville Coffee House because they can't seem to get the milk/coffee proportion right for my liking, but I'm a firm believer in patronizing neighborhood establishments and I've learned that if they use half and half instead of regular milk it cuts the acidity of the coffee. Realizing I had a dilemma on my hands, I had just crossed the street and puzzled what I should do with the dogs. There weren't many people at the counter inside, so I looped the end of the leash around one of the dull spikes of the wrought-iron fence surrounding the neighboring lawn and ran inside to place my order, making sure to keep an eye out for the dogs through the window. When I returned several minutes later, latte in hand, I discovered my canine friends had made a new acquaintance; a little old man with white hair and bright blue eyes had stooped to pet them and – much to their delight – was feeding them sugar cookies.

I approached and said hello, to which the elderly gentleman straightened up and said he hoped I didn't mind his feeding the dogs. When I responded that it didn't bother me (or the dogs) at all, he remarked that he "used to have a little schnauzer over at the old infirmary on Sixth Street, and she used to love sugar cookies." Rocky, hearing the magic word, barked a stubborn little growl on cue that let us know he was waiting for the rest of the cookies. Bess, not one to bother with formalities, pushed herself up on her hind legs and started pawing the air around the remaining sugar cookies. I, on the other hand, had started to tremble at the thought that I might be getting my first big break in the story. "You don't mean *Jennie Casseday's Free Infirmary...for Women*, do you?" I asked, trying to sound nonchalant. "Yes, that's what they called it before they converted it to apartments," he responded. I held my breath and tried not to look excited. "Say," I ventured, "did you ever experience anything strange when you were living there?"

He had gone back down on his haunches and let the dogs finish the treats in his hand. When I asked the question he looked up and thought for a second. "Well, I lived there for quite a few years when I was much younger, and I did see some *strange* things. This is a kooky neighborhood, you know," he said. "There are some *strange* characters out there, that's for sure." He studied me for a moment or two, and it seemed that his eyes had a certain mischievous sparkle to them. He patted Bess on the head and stood up again. "Yes," he laughed, "I witnessed many a strange thing over there, and just in case you were wondering, *that place is haunted as the dickens.*" I invited him to some coffee, and we sat down at one of the wrought-iron tables in front of the cafe while he told me his story.

Jack Conger rented a couple of rooms at 1412 South Sixth Street after he returned from duty in World War II in the late 1940s. Just twenty-five years old, he had a year of studies left, and hoped to finish them at the nearby University of Louisville. He recalls it as a carefree period in his life that afforded him a certain amount of leisure time and comfort, although his existence was far from a luxurious one. Unlike many young men at that time, Jack didn't have to work because his parents could afford to give him a modest monthly allowance to pay for food and rent. He spent most of his days reading or strolling around the neighborhood, where he'd make frequent stops at his favorite cafes and bars. In the evenings he liked to take in a movie or listen to the radio in his comfortable, yet sparsely furnished living room. That is, if he found himself at home after dark... Jack Conger says strange things happened at 1412 South Sixth Street when the sun went down.

The first incident he recalls happened one night after returning from a night out with some friends on Fourth Avenue. "I had moved in about three months before, and to my knowledge, there was nothing unusual about my place," he remembers. "It was sort of boring to be there alone by myself all the time, so I spent as much time out and about as I could. We had been to a movie downtown, and after stopping for a bite to eat, I came home." Jack says he turned the radio on and listened to some classical music while leafing through a magazine. An hour or so later, he became tired and decided that he wanted to go to bed. He stood up, turned off the radio and went to the bathroom to brush his teeth before going to bed.

"I was brushing my teeth," he explains, "standing there at the sink in front of the mirror when I realized music was still coming from the radio. I figured I must have forgotten to turn it off, so I went out there to turn it off, and lo and behold, it was turned off already! But I could still hear classical piano music plain as day." He turned the knobs off again, but music could still be heard, so he reached down and pulled the plug from the wall. A steady stream of classical tunes still seemed to emanate from the radio, and he could even hear the apparent hiss and crackle of static. "I just stood there and stared at the radio, and it just kept going on and on," he says, "till it finally just sort of faded away about five minutes later. I finished brushing my teeth and then went to bed as if nothing had happened. I thought if I ignored it, it wouldn't happen again."

But it did happen again, only a week or so after the first incident, and in much the same way as the time before. He had turned off the radio, or so he thought, and returned to the living room to shut it off again. As happened the time before, he stood there staring at the unplugged device while various melodies poured out, until they eventually faded away. He resumed his nightly routine and prepared for bed, hoping he would be able to ignore the radio's odd behavior. As he walked to the bedroom, however, he realized he could still hear the music. When he returned to the living room, it became apparent that the radio had started up again. He waited, and it eventually started to fade, so he turned off the floor lamp that stood next to it and hopped into bed. Once in bed, he turned off the small light on his bedside table and rolled over to go to sleep. As he lay on his side and looked through his bedroom door to the living room, however, he noticed a bright light filled the space.

He returned to the living room, relieved to hear nothing coming from the radio, but strangely puzzled about the light. He reached down and slid the switch on the cord, but the lamp would not go off. As with the radio, when he pulled the plug out of its socket on the wall, the bulb refused to go out. He just stared at it, and in a few minutes it started to fade and then went out all together. Still convinced he could ignore it, he went into his bedroom, shut the door and slept facing the other direction so he wouldn't notice any light if it came back on again. From then on he tried to avoid the living room altogether, and entered only when necessity dictated. The strange force in the living room, however, would not be ignored.

After several weeks of doing his best to disregard the strange antics of the radio and floor lamp in the living room, Jack awoke one night from a deep sleep, startled out of his slumber by a strange noise outside his bedroom. As he lay there and listened, he discerned what sounded like a long, mournful moan – perhaps female – coming from the living room. It started out soft and quiet, and then slowly crescendoed to a higher, more intense pitch before fading to what seemed to be gentle sobs. Once it faded to almost inaudible weeping, there would be a moment or two of silence, and then the strange cries would start all over again. This went on and on for almost two hours according to the alarm clock on his night table, yet he refused to get out of bed and check for the source of the odd moans. In another half hour they stopped altogether and the living room grew deathly quiet, leaving him with nothing more than a rash of goose bumps to prove that he had not imagined the whole event.

For the next several nights, the same scenario played out in his living room at 1412 South Sixth Street. Loud sobs and moaning would wake him from his sleep, and he would lie there for hours as he listened to what amounted to mournful pleas and almost painful groans. Sometimes he could hear the radio as it rapidly switched from station to station, its volume fluctuating between high and low, or the frequency cutting in and out as the light from the floor lamp flashed on and off. Although he admits that it was very unnerving, Jack says he never really felt afraid or concerned for his safety. Rather, he felt sorry for whatever being made the pitiful noises. He had the impression that a woman in distress or great sorrow had invaded his living room, a sorrowful and disembodied voice the only tangible proof of her existence.

It seemed the more he tried to ignore the sad pleading and groans, the more insistent and frequent they became. After another week of the nocturnal sobbing, the moans started to take on an almost fevered, hysterical pitch and within a fortnight they had erupted into obvious screams. When this finally happened, Jack realized he couldn't take it any longer and jumped out of bed to confront the invisible intruder. He ran into the living room and found himself totally alone, save for the radio, the floor lamp and some other furnishings, not surprised to see that radio and lamp were working overtime. A loud stream of static mixed with a whirr of voices crackled from the transmitter, and the light bulb seemed to pulsate and glow with energy surges of varying strengths.

He was more than shocked, however, when first the radio and then the lamp slowly lifted off the ground and levitated in front of him.

The hair on his arms and the back of his neck stood on end as he froze and stared at the objects floating in front of him. The air about him seemed charged with electricity, and he felt a faint tremble in the floorboards beneath. After what seemed an eternity, the lamp and the radio settled back down in their places and then slowly started their levitations again. The whole time he stood and watched, says Jack, he could hear the sorrowful moans and hysterical screams of a woman in pain, apparently emanating from the same spot as the two floating pieces of furniture. Completely overwhelmed by the sights and sounds around him, the only reaction he could muster made him flee the house and search for calm out of doors. He decided to take a prolonged walk around the neighborhood.

The next day Jack Conger decided he needed to do something.

Granted, the various items randomly floating around his living room had at last settled down by the time he returned from his walk, but he knew that the daylight offered only a temporary respite from the supernatural activity plaguing his small apartment. He couldn't shake the feeling that he had more in store than just weird sounds and antigravitational phenomena. He knew quite a few people who believed in ghosts and spirits, but he didn't really know of anyone who could help him get rid of them. He decided therefore to pay a visit to his local priest.

Father Joe, as Jack called him, had known the Congers as long as they could recall and he had served in the same downtown church for years. An eternally cheerful man with ruddy cheeks and a kind disposition, the priest had a difficult time nonetheless believing in ghosts, so he did little to mask his scepticism as he listened to Jack's account of the unexplained phenomena. "But, Jack," he insisted, "I'm telling, you there is *no such thing* as ghosts! There has to be a logical explanation for what you've seen." Although he refused to accept the possibility of earthbound spirits or any type of supernatural activity in Jack's apartment, he agreed to call the young man the next day and set up a time when he could stop by and officially bless the apartment. Relieved that he had at least shared his strange secret with someone else, Jack returned home and kept himself busy till darkness fell. He met some friends at a nearby bowling alley and didn't make his way back home until the wee hours of the morning. Fortunately, he fell fast asleep as soon as his head hit the pillow, and any would-be happenings in the next room failed to rouse him. The next morning he awoke, had coffee and donuts at a diner around the corner and then called Father Joe.

"You live *where?*" the priest repeated when Jack give his address as 1412 South Sixth Street. From the tone in his voice, the young man could tell that the father had been taken by surprise. "You mean the *old infirmary?*" he demanded after Jack repeated the address. "They took that place and turned it into apartments?" He sounded somewhat incredulous. Before the younger man had a chance to respond, the priest said he'd be right over and hung up the phone.

An hour later, both men stood in Jack's living room and surveyed the field of supernatural activity. The radio and the floor lamp rested in their spots next to the wall and didn't so much as move an inch. Although he refused to divulge any information on the matter, Father

Joe appeared to be a bit unnerved, and Jack felt sure the priest knew something about the apartment at 1412 South Sixth Street that he chose not to share. He placed a small leather valise on the table and unpacked several items including a small vile of holy water, a Bible and a brass crucifix. He draped a vestment over his shoulders and quickly made his way from room to room, cross held out in front as he flicked holy water and recited a rapid succession of prayers in Latin. When he had finished, he packed his things and said his good-byes, refusing Jack's invitation to stay for a glass of wine or cup of coffee.

That very evening Jack found himself in the kitchen off of the living room preparing a light dinner before he headed to a friend's house for a game night. He had just scrambled three large eggs and watched them slowly cook and sizzle in a large cast iron skillet laden with butter, when a strange sensation suddenly overcame him. A chill ran down his spine, and he found it very difficult to breathe, almost as if a heavy weight had been placed on his chest. He looked towards the living room and realized that dusk had fallen. As if forced and prodded by a pair of invisible hands, he reluctantly walked into the parlor as a sense of dread settled over him. His throat constricted for a moment, and he thought he might choke to death.

As he had feared, the radio and the lamp levitated inches above the surfaces they rested on, and they both started to rotate before his eyes. The dial on the radio started spinning around and a blur of static and unidentifiable voices punctuated the air at the same time the light bulb flashed on and off. He could also hear the plaintive cries and sobbing screams that had filled the room before, but this time they seemed more distressed and pained than before. Immobilized, he stared at the objects in the air before him and gulped for air, afraid he might suffocate if not able to rally himself from that spot. His head started to spin, and he grew faint, but whatever appeared to have a hold over him suddenly released itself and allowed him to breathe freely. At that very same moment a strange white mist started to fill the room, and the room seemed to experience a drastic drop in temperature.

Jack also noted a rapid rise in the humidity level about him, and he realized beads of moisture had started to accumulate on the wall behind the radio and floor lamp. In a matter of seconds, it seemed that a dense, white fog had blanketed the room and he could just barely make out the shapes of the two floating items as they settled back down to their original locations. Then he heard an almost muted pitter-patter and felt something soft hit his head. He looked up and realized that it had started to rain in his own living room! When he heard the water droplets start falling at a more rapid pace, he shook himself and then bolted for the street. Once outside, he quickly sought out a pay phone and called Father Joe.

An assistant at the parish house answered and informed him that the priest had gone to St. Louis for personal reasons and didn't plan to return for several days. At a loss, Jack Conger hung up the phone and checked into the nearby Marquette Terrace hotel. He decided at that moment that he would not set foot in his apartment again unless someone else accompanied him or until the strange powers in his living room vacated the premises. That night he slept his first dreamless sleep in months, and when he rose the next morning he actually felt invigorated and refreshed. He called a cousin, and together they went to the apartment at 1412 South Sixth Street and retrieved some of his clothes. As they entered the living room, he noticed pools of water—unevaporated despite the soaring summer temperatures outside—from the day before that had collected on the floor and on the tabletops. Pushing it out of his mind, he returned to his room at the hotel and waited for Father Joe's return.

More than a week passed, and although the priest had indeed arrived safely back in town, he neglected to return any of Jack's calls. Puzzled, the young man decided to wait another day or two and then find the priest himself if he didn't hear back from him. Granted, he received a comfortable allowance from his parents, but it by no means meant he could afford to spend weeks at a time in a hotel. He needed to get back into his apartment, and he saw Father Joe as his only remedy for the situation at hand. And after the last weird occurrences in the living room, he definitely had no intention of being there on his own. As a matter of fact, he had gone so far as to call the landlord and see about getting out of his lease, but the old woman had refused, calling his sanity into question when he mentioned the strange things he had witnessed.

When Sunday rolled around without a call back from the priest, Jack Conger decided he needed to go to Mass. He sat through the service and made sure to be one of the last to leave the church; that way Father Joe would have to talk to him. When the old man saw him approach, the look in his eyes betrayed the fact that he had been avoiding further contact with Jack.

"Oh... I was afraid you'd hunt me down," the priest confessed. "I was hoping my little prayers had taken care of your problems." Embarrassed, he wrung his hands and looked down at his feet.

"Taken *care* of my problems?" Jack repeated sarcastically. "It got *worse* after you left." He studied the man in front of him for a moment, and then softened his tone. "Father Joe," he said gently, "it's *me*...Jack Conger. You've known my family for ages, and I've got a real problem here and I need your help. I don't know what else to do!" He stopped for a second and waited for the priest to react. Seeing that no response was forthcoming, he shrugged his shoulders and sighed. "I don't want to cause any trouble for you, I swear, but I just don't know what to do...I'm sorry."

At that, the priest looked up and took the young man by the shoulders. "No," he said with a gentle shake of the head, "*I'm the one who should be sorry.*" He led Jack to the front of the church and told him to stay put; the priest had a couple matters to attend to, but he told Jack he'd be back shortly. They would talk more then.

Twenty minutes later, the priest emerged through a small wooden door and found Jack sitting in the first row of pews, somewhat lost in thought. He approached the young man and sat down next to him, his leather valise still tucked under one arm. "Now, then," the older man chuckled, "I've got a confession *for you*." He slid in a little closer and handed Jack a small, leather-bound book with the title HOLY RITES OF EXORCISM emblazoned across the front in red letters. "Remember how I said there is no such thing as ghosts and stuff?" he asked. "Well, I guess I lied..."

More confused than ever, Jack just held the book and stared. "I don't get it," he said. "What's this all about? Does *this* have something to do with the strange things going on in my apartment?" He used his index finger to point at the book in his hand. "I got the impression that you knew something you weren't telling me, but now I'm totally in the dark." He watched the priest slowly stand up and motion for him to follow. They walked outside into the bright sunshine and started off in the direction of 1412 South Sixth Street. By the time they reached their destination a half hour later, Jack Conger would get an earful about the haunting at his Sixth Street apartment.

Father Joe initially had not revealed to him that he had already paid several visits to the gray-shingled building on Sixth Street by the time Jack contacted him. The first times, he related, had been over fifty years before when they still used it as an infirmary. Even though Casseday had been a strict Methodist, many of her clients were poor Catholic women, and the priest was often called upon for various services, including baptisms and – very often – the administering of last rites. The last two times had been in the decade before World War II, when he had been called in to investigate various *disturbances* at the Sixth Street property. Since then, he had hoped he wouldn't have to pay any more visits to the old clinic, but when he learned that Jack Conger was living in the old building he was overcome with a sense of dread. As the two men strolled down the sunny streets, the priest shared more of the details.

Jack Conger, as it were, happened to be living in the part of the infirmary that used to serve as the maternity ward, an area that saw no small share of pain, suffering and death on the part of its patients. The priest could recall that on one weekend alone in 1929 he gave the last rites to four women who died in childbirth, and he could still hear the torment of their screams in his ears, as if it were yesterday. Then there was the influenza epidemic in 1918; he couldn't even keep track of how many women perished that month. Although he was a skeptic, he wasn't at all surprised when rumors started surfacing about awful screams and strange visions when the place was completely empty. Jack's living room, he said, at one time had two beds in it, set aside especially for the most severe cases. As a consequence, quite a few women met their unfortunate ends in that very room. The odd occurrences seemed to be a result of that sad connection.

Both men stood and examined the room. Nothing looked out of the ordinary, save for a few puddles of water slowly evaporating on the floor directly in front of the floor lamp. Next to it, on a wooden end table, sat the radio in silence. The priest pointed to the wall behind it and said the two beds he mentioned usually stood perpendicular to the wall in that very spot with their headboards touching it. Other than that area, he knew of no other part of the house where strange things were said to happen. Turning to look at Jack, he said "I still don't believe in ghosts and all that stuff, but I have to admit that I cannot logically explain any of the things I've witnessed in this room. I've seen some odd things, mind you, but in my entire career as a man of the cloth, this is the only time I couldn't explain it away." He set the leather valise on the couch and extracted the book of exorcism rites, turning it over in his hand as he stood next the young man. "Granted, the church does teach us about the occult and things of that nature, but most of us nowadays think it's pretty *old school.* We live in the modern age now, don't we?"

Jack Conger stood and stared at the priest, shaking his head in disbelief. He could hardly believe what he was hearing. Father Joe had known about the strange happenings in his apartment. He didn't know if he was more relieved that someone could actually vouch for his story or more concerned that the priest had not been able to eliminate the supernatural events. When he asked the older man what they should do, the priest replied that they would wait until dark and try to convince the strange force to leave – just as he had done on two separate occasions in the past. He hoped this time it would not return.

Several hours later the two men were standing in the same spot in the room as the last of the light outside gave way to the gray shadows creeping across the floor towards the lamp and the radio. The priest had laid out the crucifix and the holy water and he held the opened exorcism book in his hands. As he had already explained to Jack, priests usually used the rites of exorcism to cast demons and evil spirits from human bodies, but in this case some of the ancient rituals outlined in the book would serve to confront the entities present in the old infirmary. He started to read a liturgy in Latin and out of the corner of his eye he kept a close watch on the young protégé at his side.

Jack Conger recalls standing there and watching for what seemed like hours, but looking back, he figures it was probably more like an hour or forty-five minutes. He had started to relax a bit and began to wonder if anything would happen. No sooner had he let down his guard when the crucifix on the small end table next to him suddenly lifted a foot into the air and shot across the room as if hurled by an invisible hand. Although he had started to tremble, the young man noticed that the priest kept on with his liturgy as if nothing had happened. Several minutes after that, beads of condensed moisture started to collect on the wall in front of the two men and then trickled slowly downwards as a faint rumble started to shake the ground beneath them.

As the vibration in the floor increased and spread to the walls and ceiling overhead, the light in the lamp started to flicker on and off and then buzzed into a bright glow. At the same time, a staticky crackle filled the room as the radio came to life and randomly switched from station to station. A misty fog started to rise from the floor, and the lamp and radio both simultaneously lifted off the ground and floated as a blanket of cool moisture seemed to envelope the two men. Water droplets fell from the ceiling, and the brass crucifix that had shot across the room before now reappeared in front of the priest, apparently suspended in mid air as it rotated on its vertical axis just inches from the man's nose. The walls seemed to shake, and a low wail surrounded the two men, barely audible at first, but then expanding into a powerful, pleading scream.

Apparently unperturbed, the priest continued his prayers as the moaning increased and sent reverberations through the floor and ceiling. The fog in the room seemed to become denser, and as he concentrated on the sounds about him, Jack realized that more than one voice could be heard. It sounded like three or four female voices, all of them crying out in agony as the volume and pitch increased and threatened to drown out the voice of the priest. The light bulb in the lamp died, and it seemed that a dense shroud of blackness had been lowered inside the room. Only a small ball of hazy, pulsating, blue light hung in the air before the two men, its radiance fading to almost nothing then surging to blinding brilliance as the cross danced in the air around it.

As the intensity of the moans grew, so did the size of the ball of light, and within several minutes it had assumed the size of a human figure. Jack Conger and Father Joe looked on as the vague form of a woman materialized before them, flanked on either side by two other forms that appeared to be female as well. The light shimmered and flickered, and faint features began to appear on the three faces staring at them, eventually revealing mouths opened wide in a tortured scream. His heart pounding in his ears, Jack watched the three ghostly figures hover before him, the agony in their disembodied voices at a crescendo as the priest continued the methodical recitation of his prayers.

Horrified, Jack could only stand and stare as his brain attempted to process a barrage of information. Although he had never actually seen a ghost before, he was quite convinced that he was beholding the ghosts or spirits of three women, and they seemed to want to tell him something. Sadness overcame the young man as he watched the lifeless forms hovering and wailing before him, and although the eyes were nothing more than mere gray ovals, he sensed that they were looking to him for something, almost pleading, as it were. The priest finished his prayers and addressed the vague, silvery forms in English, telling them they were free to leave this realm and move onto the next. He repeated this several times, and when Jack realized it was not providing the desired effect, he added: "Your babies are fine. You can go on now. Your children are fine." With that, the awful moaning stopped, and the figures started to fade and then quickly vanished all together, leaving the two men standing alone in silence in the dark living room.

"I guess it hit me, all of a sudden like, that they were worried about their babies," recalls Jack of that night. "All they needed to hear was that their children were fine. When they heard that, it released them, I guess." Jack Conger says he and his friend, Father Joe, retired to the kitchen after that and drank coffee and talked till the sun came up the next morning. After that day, Jack says he never had any problems with supernatural activity in his living room. He lived at 1412 South Sixth Street for almost two years after that, and the radio and floor lamp only came on when he turned them on.

ABOUT THE CABBAGE PATCH

When Louise Marshall founded the Cabbage Patch Settlement House in 1910, Old Louisville had already reached its apex as the premier residential neighborhood in the city. Just steps from the grand mansions of Saint James Court and Third and Fourth Avenues, however, a large portion of the local population lived in less than modest circumstances. One lower-class neighborhood bordering the elegant boundaries

The generous spirit of famed Victorian writer Alice Hegan Rice reportedly makes occasional appearances at the Old Louisville Charity she helped make famous. It sits across the street from the old Jennie Casseday's Free Infirmary for Women.

of Louisville's first suburb, the Cabbage Patch, would give rise to one of Victorian America's most enduring legacies, *Mrs. Wiggs of the Cabbage Patch*. Written in 1901 by Alice Hegan Rice, a noted local author who lived at 1444 Saint James Court, it eventually hit the stage and came to life in at least three film adaptations.

Today, however, this one-time best seller has been largely forgotten. Although immensely popular in the year of its publication, and for many years afterward with each subsequent printing, the book met with mixed critical response, especially in regard to its handling of class and socioeconomic conflict. In an almost Dickensian tale of adversity, perseverance and triumph, the heroine and single mother of five, Mary Wiggs, struggles to maintain her family in a shantytown near the railroad tracks.

The author, Alice Caldwell Hegan, was born in 1870 in nearby Shelbyville, Kentucky, but grew up in Louisville, where she enjoyed a somewhat privileged upbringing. After completing her education, she undertook social and philanthropic work in the city, working closely with the families in the slums of the Cabbage Patch district. Her novel drew heavily on those experiences in the Cabbage Patch, and for the rest of her life she remained an ardent proponent for the rights of the underprivileged. She married Cale Rice, another noted writer, the year after publication of "Mrs. Wiggs," and they lived in Louisville until her death in 1942. Known for the intimate soirees and elegant to-do's in their stately 1910 mansion on Saint James Court, the couple was said to be devoted to each other. Cale Rice committed suicide less than a year after his wife's death.

Although the body of Alice Hegan Rice rests at nearby Cave Hill Cemetery, rumors persist that her spirit – and that of her beloved husband – refuse to leave the elegant lanes and shady sidewalks of their favorite neighborhood. Not too long after Rice's tragic suicide in 1943, neighbors reported strange glowing lights and unexplained flashes in the couple's bedroom windows, when no one was supposedly in that room. On other occasions, visitors to the house heard what sounded like festive party music from the 1920s and the unintelligible din of voices; however, when they searched for the source, they were never able to find anything. One neighbor even claims that he looked out his front window in the 1950s and saw an elegantly dressed lady from the Roaring Twenties slowly stroll down the sidewalk and then vanish into thin air as she reached the front steps of the Rice House. Although the gentleman admits that he did not know the Rices, he claims that the woman he saw could have been the spitting image of Alice Hegan Rice, based on photographs taken of her in the 1920s.

A similar figure has also been spotted at the present site of the Cabbage Patch Settlement House, across the road from Jennie Casseday's Infirmary in a series of modest shotgun houses at 1413 South Sixth Street. Several volunteers claim to have looked up from their desks at various times in the evening and spied the apparition of a middle-aged woman gazing serenely back at them before slowly fading away. Although some have referred to this apparition as that of Mrs. Wiggs, it is not known for sure if there was indeed an actual Mrs. Wiggs of the Cabbage Patch. Most prefer to believe it is the ghost of Alice Hegan Rice herself, coming back to check on the institution inspired by one of her most enduring characters.

Chapter 5

CONRAD-CALDWELL HOUSE

What starts out as a leisurely fifteen-minute stroll through the streets and alleyways of the country's largest Victorian neighborhood can easily turn into an adventure that lasts several hours or the whole day. For many people, this journey has become a permanent odyssey. For lifelong residents and first-time visitors alike in Old Louisville, this colorful neighborhood offers a steady stream of surprises and secrets to those who take the time to explore it. A treasure trove of architectural splendor and forgotten history, Old Louisville stands out as something special in the nation and in the state of Kentucky. Although somewhat slowly perhaps, the inhabitants of the city of Louisville itself have also come to realize that no other place in the city can surpass this area for its wealth of charm, elegance and nostalgia. Within the boundaries of historic Old Louisville, however, Saint James Court stands out among all the other neighborhoods for its grassy, gas-lit boulevard, splashing fountain and picture-perfect homes. And on elegant Saint James Court, one magnificent mansion at 1402 stands out as the most impressive residence: The Conrad-Caldwell House.

Known as the finest home in the city for many years, this massive Bedford limestone construction in the Richardsonian Romanesque style still counts as one of the most stunning homes in Old Louisville. When Theophilus Conrad, a Frenchman from Alsace who made his Louisville fortune in the tanning business, hired famed local architect Arthur Loomis to design the mansion in the 1890s, the city had already established itself in the new "West" as a comfortable enclave noted for its lavish homes. In 1831, traveler Caleb Atewar commented on a recent trip to Louisville, then just barely in its fourth decade of existence, that "[t]here are probably more ease and affluence in this place, than in any other western town – their houses are splendid, substantial, and richly furnished; and I saw more large mirrors in their best rooms, than I saw anywhere else. Paintings and mirrors adorn the walls, and all the furniture is splendid and costly." With this in mind, Conrad set out to maintain the city's reputation and impress his neighbors.

The original construction price was set at $35,000, and within weeks all eyes in the city had turned to the large corner lot on Saint James Court where work on the "Castle" had begun. Within several months local workers and stone masons had erected a huge stone shell replete with gargoyles, floral swags, massive arches and elaborate decorative motifs that towered over everything else on the court. After another several months had passed, craftsmen started to embellish the interior with the finest appointments money could buy. Beautiful stained glass and elaborately carved woodwork in the balustrade and wainscoting along the stairway and balcony graced the magnificent front staircase. The interior also features the fleur-de-lis, the stylized iris from heraldry that is itself a symbol of Louisville. The most opulent room in the house, the parlor, featured woodwork of birds-eye maple, and in other rooms off the entry hall, ornate chandeliers, carved paneling, crown molding and intricate parquet floors offered just a glimpse of the abundant detail yet to be discovered throughout the rest of the house.

Although the house has been run as a museum since 1987, tour guides at the Conrad-Caldwell House don't recommend that you wander off and try to explore the lavish interiors on your own. It seems that a former resident of the stately home doesn't appreciate strangers snooping around unattended in *his* house...even though he died and left the premises a century ago. At the beautiful Conrad-Caldwell House there have been more than just a few reports of curious individuals getting more than they bargained for when trying to sneak off and explore by themselves. In the mid 1990s a lady visitor did just that, however, when she slipped away from her group and decided to poke her head through a door into a third-floor room that had been closed for restoration. Several moments later she ran screaming down the stairway past her friends and refused to go back up to the third floor. When asked what had upset her so, she would only reply that she had seen "a mean little man from the olden days, shaking his raised index finger" at her in admonition. The terrified woman also reported that she knew the man wasn't real because she had seen right through the apparition to the wood paneling on the other side of the room.

Theories abound as to the source of this ghostly figure seen on various occasions, but many feel that some of the sightings involve none other than Theophilus Conrad himself. Reputedly a stern taskmaster, associates knew Conrad as a hard worker and no-nonsense kind of person, despite the wealth and prestige he had accumulated. While other mansions in the neighborhood usually employed an entire staff of live-in servants, the frugal Conrads made due with several "dailies" who came in every morning and took care of the cooking, cleaning and gardening. Although he wasn't a big man, he nonetheless carried himself like a giant and demanded the respect of his family and employees. By all accounts, Conrad was indeed the king of his castle.

Several other visitors have reported seeing a short man in the billiard room as well, and curiously enough, he always seems to manifest himself to those who wander off and try to explore the house on their own. "He looked like the man in the picture I saw," reported one tourist after an unsettling encounter with the little man in the billiard room in 1995. The man in the picture he referred to was none other than Theo Conrad himself.

On one occasion, two newlyweds had just held their wedding reception at the opulent mansion, and as they filed down the walkway through the throng of family and friends, they looked up and noticed a gentleman "in an old-fashioned tweed suit" smoking a cigar on a third floor balcony. Neither the new bride nor her groom recognized the little man, so the woman asked her mother about the unknown guest's identity. But when they looked up, he had already vanished, and a thorough search of the house turned up nothing but the pleasant aroma of cigar smoke in the former billiard room. Coincidentally enough, the balcony

A Richardsonian Romanesque masterpiece of stone, the Conrad-Cadwell House has stood watch over lovely Saint James Court for more than 100 years.

where the man had been spotted was known as the smoking balcony, a small outdoor area connected to the billiard room where gentlemen could enjoy their tobacco after a game of snooker.

Elizabeth Stith seems to think the descriptions of the gentleman in the third-floor pool room fit the description of Mr. Caldwell, the second King of the Castle, rather than Mr. Conrad, who died in 1905. The Caldwell family purchased the huge house on Saint James Court and lived there for thirty-five years. After the Saint James Court Historic Foundation purchased the home in 1987 and restored it for use as a museum, Ms. Stith served as director of the house museum for a time. If anyone would know details of the former residents of the Conrad-Caldwell House, she would be the one. During her seven years as director, she conducted numerous hours of research and investigation about the house and the families that had lived there. "That description sounds like Mr. Caldwell," she explains. "He was a very short man. And the billiard room wasn't added to the house until after he and his family moved in." She points out that Mr. Caldwell died in the house as well. He reportedly spent many hours with his gentlemen friends in his favorite room of the house, the billiard room on the third floor.

According to Elizabeth, Mrs. Caldwell designed the present-day billiards room and added the cabinets for the cue sticks and billiard balls in the early 1900s. "She really loved this house, and she put a lot of work into it. When the Caldwells moved in, she redecorated the mansion and gave it the feel it has today. She got many of the ideas while traveling abroad." Elizabeth points out that Mrs. Caldwell also died in the house, illness confining her to her second-floor bedroom for the last couple years of her life. Even though the prominent Louisville socialite died many years ago, there are those who feel she hasn't quite left the lovely house she adored on Saint James Court, Elizabeth Stith included.

"I get the impression she wants to make sure we're taking good care of her home," the former director explains, recalling a strange encounter she had one February evening. "It was six o'clock, so it was dark at that time already, and I was there alone." She needed to turn off the lights before leaving, and as she made her way down the grand stairway from the third floor, an odd shape appeared on the steps. "It was down by the grandfather clock, and I noticed a white, milky form, almost like a veil hanging there. I couldn't really make out a definite shape or anything. It was more like a patch of something foggy just hanging there." Not quite sure if her eyes were playing tricks on her, Elizabeth tried to maintain her composure as she made her way around the odd shape and down the stairs.

"Somewhere in the back of my mind I remembered what someone had once told me," she recalls, "that when things manifest themselves like that, they just want to be acknowledged. So I tried to acknowledge it." Elizabeth then continued with her business and told the strange form that everything in the house was fine and that she "was just turning out the lights." Elizabeth says the figure eventually faded and disappeared completely, but not without leaving behind an extremely cold spot on the steps. Coincidentally enough, many people have reported a mysterious cold spot on that very portion of the stairs.

Deb Riall has taken over as the current director of the Conrad-Caldwell House museum, and although she herself has not witnessed any apparitions or such, she has heard stories from other people who have. She can also recall one occurrence that "was definitely odd." Deb had gone to the kitchen to heat up her lunch in the microwave and found herself at the sink, waiting for the timer to go off. "I was standing near the sink," she explains, "when I looked down and noticed the little drain basket on the counter. It was rocking back and forth, from side to side, very slowly and deliberately. I just kept staring at it, waiting for it to eventually stop, but it just kept going back and forth..." At that point she remembered the same thing that Elizabeth Stith had: *They just want to be acknowledged.* In a loud and clear voice, she said "OK...I know you're here" and looked around the room. Although she didn't see anything, she looked down and noticed the drain basket as it stopped rocking back and forth. "I slammed the microwave door a couple times, I leaned on the counter," she explains, "but I was never able to get the drain basket to move like that again. I don't know what it was." Was Mrs. Caldwell trying to get her attention?

Some think that the former lady of the house can be very vociferous if she needs to. A former housekeep recollects an incident several years ago that made her think so. It was late summer, in the afternoon, and a storm had just blown in and darkened the neighborhood as she cleaned the stairs in the front of the house. It began to thunder loudly, and then large drops of rain started to fall and splash against the windows. "It happened so fast," the woman recalls, "that I didn't even notice anything till I looked up and saw how black it was outside." No sooner had she noticed the rain coming down in torrents, she claims, than a woman's voice frantically called from the third floor that *"the windows are open!"* The housekeeper ran up to the top floor of the house to discover that someone had indeed left the windows open, and she quickly closed them before more rain came in and did any serious damage. "I'm

A lovely oil portrait of Grace Caldwell hangs in an elegant front parlor in the Conrad-Caldwell House.

Mrs. Caldwell redesigned many rooms in the Conrad-Caldwell House — this study on the first floor included— after a visit to Europe in the early 1900s.

photos with permission of Conrad-Caldwell House

An oil portrait of the stern Mr. Caldwell waits at the bottom of the grand stairway in the opulent Conrad-Caldwell House.

A carved wooden fleur-de-lis graces the intricate ballus trade of the main staircase in the largest home on St. James Court. The fleur-de-lis is the symbol of Louisville.

pretty sure it was Mrs. Caldwell," she remarked. "She's always watching out for her house."

Aside from the grand front stairway, some people sense that Mrs. Caldwell exerts a very strong presence in the home's butler's pantry as well. A small storage room off the dining room that connected to the pantry and the kitchen, the original inhabitants of the house used this area to store their best china and serving items. A very typical feature in nicer Victorian homes, these small rooms served as the last stop for food on the way to the dinner table. After the cook prepared the dish in the kitchen, it would be brought to the butler's pantry where it could be kept warm and then arranged and formally presented for serving. Many of the homes in Old Louisville still have the original butler's pantries, and like most, the one at the Conrad-Caldwell House has various cabinets and drawers used to store tablecloths, napkins, cutlery and stemware in addition to a large table used for plating dishes between courses. The pantry in the Conrad-Caldwell House has one thing, however, that lets visitors know that they haven't entered just any run-of-the-mill butler's pantry. A tall, narrow, wooden door opens to reveal a tall, narrow, metal safe used to hide some of the most valuable silver in all of Old Louisville. This could explain why former employees say Mrs. Caldwell's presence has always been "exceptionally strong" in the butler's pantry.

Often described as a woman with impeccable taste, Mrs. Caldwell reportedly prided herself on setting a lovely table for family and friends. She often supervised the selection of courses for elegant meals and she always insisted on using the best table linens, bone ware, crystal and silver for her meals. She could often be seen in the butler's pantry, fussing about before meals, and she herself would unlock the safe and extract the choicest silver items to deck the table. Her neighbors reported that she could turn an ordinary afternoon tea into the most elegant of affairs. Maybe this is why an unexplained cold spot in the room has been experienced on numerous occasions, often right before elegant weddings or lavish meals held on the premises.

"I hope she was just checking on things!" says a former bride who hosted her wedding reception in the house several years ago. "I was standing by myself in the little pantry room off the dining room, right in front of where the safe is, when all of a sudden I was surrounded by an ice-cold blast of air!" she recalls. "I looked up and around me, because

I thought the air-conditioning had just come on and was blowing at me through a vent, but I didn't see anything at all. Then I got this *very strange* feeling like someone was watching me or something, and I knew I was not alone in that room."

Perhaps one of the strangest encounters with the former Mrs. Caldwell – if that's indeed who it is – happened several years ago during preparations for another wedding at the house. The groom's sister, a self-described no-nonsense kind of woman from Salt Lake City, had just flown in, and she and some family friends had gone to the mansion to decorate for the ceremony the next afternoon. "It was about nine in the evening, and it was very dark outside," she explains. "It seemed like none of the streetlights were working. There were five of us all together, and we were decorating the grand stairway with flowers and ribbons. I was at the very bottom of the steps, and the others were on the second-floor landing." The woman says she looked up from what she was doing and noticed at eye level a spoon not more than three feet in front of her. "It was just floating in the air!" she says. "A beautiful old-fashioned silver spoon, all ornate and stuff, just hanging in mid-air..." As she watched, the woman claims the spoon sailed through the air and landed with a clatter on the floor of the butler's pantry. "I went and found it there, lying on the floor in front of the old safe. But the safe was wide open, and I don't think it had been open when I saw it before that. I noticed there were some matching pieces of silver in the vault, so I put the spoon with them and then closed the door. Maybe the lady of the house was trying to get my attention so I'd close the door to the safe," she says. "When I told the others what had happened, they just said I had to be going crazy, but I know what I saw."

It seems that odd occurrences at the Conrad-Caldwell House don't limit themselves to encounters involving former visitors or employees and the supposed ghosts of Mr. and Mrs. Caldwell, however. After the Caldwells sold the house around the time World War II broke out, it passed to the Presbyterian Church and served for many years as a retirement home for women. Although the caretakers of the property took precautions to preserve the basic integrity of the structure, they did add on two wings that changed the original layout of the mansion. Some of this space can be rented as rooms and apartments today, and a former tenant got a little more than she bargained for one night when she and some friends pulled out a *Ouija* board.

"I lived in the back part, the new part that was built by the nursing home, and I had heard people say the old mansion had a lot of ghosts," reports Sue Larson, a former U of L student who lived there for two years. "One night I was in my room with a couple friends, just hanging out and stuff and they convinced me to let them get a *Ouija* board and play around with it." Although she "didn't believe in things like the *Ouija* board," Sue says she didn't feel threatened by it. "I thought it was perfectly harmless," she recalls. "I'd heard scary things about people who used the *Ouija* board before, but I never believed it."

By the end of that night, she wouldn't be so skeptical of other people's stories about the *Ouija* board. "We started off with simple, goofy kinds of questions. *Is anyone there? Can you hear us? Are you a woman? Are you a man?* And we'd get simple answers like YES and NO on the board, but I just assumed that someone was manipulating the pointer, so it was no big deal." The girls started to get a strange feeling, however, when they started asking more specific questions of the board. "We found out it was a girl, and when I asked her name, we got G-R-A-C-E on the board. Her favorite color was P-I-N-K. Then someone asked her what color her hair was, and she spelled A-U-B-U-R-N. " Sue says it went on and on like this for about a half an hour. When she asked the woman where she lived, the answer was H-E-R-E.

"We all got freaked out then," she says. "Especially me. I didn't want to do it anymore, but they were laughing and stuff, and not taking it too seriously, so I let them talk me into putting my hands back on the board." The girls decided to try a different vein of questioning from that point forward. "They all wanted to ask personal things about themselves to see if the spirit knew the answers. *What did I have for breakfast this morning? Who did I talk to on the phone last night? Where does my father come from?* And most of the answers were dead on!" Sue realizes that the answers to some of questions could have been common knowledge to those assembled, but she got the distinct impression that several of the answers would have been known only to the ones who had asked the questions.

"*Who made my bed this morning and yesterday?*" asked Sue, resting her finger tips on the pointer as she looked at Sarah, a quasi roommate who lived down the hall. Two days in a row, Sue had walked into her bedroom after showering and dressing to find that someone had neatly made her bed. Although there was no reason for the other girl to make her bed, Sue could only assume that her friend down the hall had done it as an unexpected act of kindness. She expected this to be borne out as she intently watched the pointer silently glide from one letter to the next. "It spelled out *I D-I-D!* Not *S-A-R-A*-H as I had anticipated!" Sue also says her shocked glance in Sarah's direction elicited nothing more than a quizzical look in return. "I asked her if she had made my bed, and she just looked at me like I was crazy and asked why she would do something she had never done before."

Sue Larson looked down at the *Ouija* board, suddenly overcome with a sense of uneasiness, and decided to ask one more question: *Why did you make my bed?* The pointer started moving slowly and spelled out this reply: B-E-C-A-U-S-E-Y-O-U-L-O-O-K-L-I-K-E-T-H-E-B-E-S-T-F-R-I-E-N-D-I-U-S-E-D-T-O-H-A-V-E-A-N-D-B-E-C-A-U-S-E-Y-O-U-A-R-E-N-I-C-E. *"Because you look like the best friend I used to have! And because you are nice!"* says Sue Larson. "That really spooked me and I made them put the board away right then and there. I haven't touched one since then, and I don't plan on it ever again. Especially after what I found out a couple of weeks after that episode."

Sue says her encounter with the spirit on the *Ouija* board was made all the more eerie several weeks afterwards. "My family was in town and wanted to get a tour of the mansion. They wanted me to go with them since I had never even done the tour, if you can believe it," she explains. "I had calmed down a bit, so I wasn't nervous anymore or anything." But when she arrived and started the guided tour with her family, she claims no more than a minute or two had passed when her sense of uneasiness returned. "The docent had just started her explanation of the formal parlor when one of the other people in the group pointed to a portrait of a young woman on the far wall. She's a young girl with brown hair done up, and she dressed nicely, and there's lots of pink in the painting that matched the pink throughout the room." According to Larson, the elderly woman wanted to know who had painted the portrait and who had been the subject. When the tour guide answered, Sue says a chill ran down her spine and reminded her of the incident with the *Ouija* board. "Oh, that's *Grace*, the Caldwell's daughter," the woman had responded.

Sue Larson says she moved to an apartment in the Highlands and hasn't been back to the Conrad-Caldwell House since. "I don't know if we really made contact with Grace Caldwell's spirit for real or not," she explains, "but it was a really weird experience for me. I don't do *Ouija* boards anymore. And if I think a house is haunted, I don't go in it!"

Is the Conrad-Caldwell House really haunted? Who can say, except the scores of people who have had strange, unexplained encounters in the lovely stone mansion on the corner of Saint James Court and Magnolia in the heart of Old Louisville?

ABOUT DUPONT SQUARE

Like much of Old Louisville, there's more to Central Park than meets the eye. Scratch the thin veneer covering the past lives of this public green space, Louisville's old DuPont Square, and you might be surprised at what you find. To see it today, with its quiet paths, towering trees and shady walkways, visitors couldn't begin to imagine the long and colorful history behind the seventeen acres of land in the heart of the Old Louisville Preservation District that comprise Central Park. Most wouldn't suspect, either, that the park is reputedly one of the most haunted locations in the city, a spot where local residents have caught fleeting glances of a shadowy figure clad in a black cape and wide-brimmed hat as it drifts about between the gas lamps. Speculations vary as to who the spectral figure might be; however, most seem to believe the apparition is none other than a member of a well-known Louisville family who died under mysterious circumstances over a century ago. But, in order to understand the circumstances around his death, one first needs to understand a little of the history behind Central Park.

Although the city has grown considerably, when settlers to the region first arrived in the late 1700s, nothing but marshes and woodlands covered the entire Old Louisville area. It wasn't until 1837 that Cuthbert Bullitt built a small log cabin used as a hunting lodge on the gentle rise that now comprises the highest ground of Central Park. Although a farmhouse also occupied the little hill for a time after that, the land remained virtually unspoiled for years. Stuart Robinson, pastor of the affluent Second Presbyterian Church, bought the land that is now Central Park in 1859; however, the Civil War broke out before he could do much with the land. The Reverend Robinson, a strong and vocal supporter of the Confederacy in a city with just as many pro-Union sentiments, fled to Canada and remained there until after the war ended. Upon his return to Louisville in the late 1860s, he began to focus his interests on his property south of town. He expanded his estate on the hill and included an Italianate country villa sometime around 1870.

The Reverend Robinson didn't spend much time in his new house in the woods, however, and sold it to one of the DuPonts in 1871. The famous DuPont family of Wilmington, Delaware, had built a financial empire on gunpowder and chemicals and counted as one of the wealthiest families in the nation. One branch of the family, Alfred Victor DuPont and his younger brother Antoine Biderman, had settled in Louisville in the late 1850s, and it seems they took a fancy to Robinson's mansion and grounds. They reportedly offered to buy it from him for an exorbitant amount, and Robinson took the money and built himself an even finer mansion just across the road. The Robinson-Landward House still stands today at the corner of Fourth and Magnolia and is recognized as one of the more impressive early homes of Old Louisville.

Alfred Victor, or "Uncle Fred" as he came to be known, acted as the patriarch of the Kentucky branch of the DuPonts. By all accounts, he cut a rather unkempt and disheveled figure, despite the large fortune under his control. Some claim this might be due to the fact that there was no Mrs. DuPont to help him maintain a neat appearance. In spite of his somewhat eccentric nature and gruff demeanor, he still had the reputation of being a dandy about town, and being an independent bachelor, Uncle Fred preferred to live in a hotel room at the old Galt House Hotel downtown. Although rumor has it that he might have built several of the grander Old Louisville mansions, he didn't live in any of them. It appears that Uncle Fred preferred certain downtown "amenities" that were harder to come by in the wilderness.

Uncle Fred's brother, Biderman, and his family lived in the former Robinson estate, and they eventually opened the front lawn to the public as a park and playground – due in no small part to the DuPonts' keen business sense. "Bid" realized that if they offered residents a green space with regular special events like concerts, fireworks and balloon ascensions, people would most likely have to use the DuPont's mule-drawn Central Passenger Railroad to get there. As a result, the park became known as DuPont Square, although Central Park appeared as the preferred name in city atlases and the City Directory.

Much of the development of Old Louisville can be attributed to the DuPonts and their proximity to today's Central Park. When the site for the grand Southern Exposition was chosen in 1883, many historians feel that it came as no coincidence that Biderman DuPont, chairman of the committee, chose a location just south of and adjacent to DuPont Square. And when he realized there was a need for more skilled labor in the neighborhood, he took action and provided the major funding for a new high school, the DuPont Manual Training School, which opened at the corner of Brook and Oak Streets.

Barely two weeks after attending the dedication ceremonies for the school in 1893, Uncle Fred suddenly died of a tragic heart attack on the porch of the Galt House Hotel. At least that's what the *Courier Journal* reported. Certain townspeople, however, liked to point out with a snicker that Alfred DuPont had indeed suffered an "awful" little heart attack.

Although many years would pass before the "truth" surfaced, it seemed to be common knowledge at that time that Uncle Fred preferred downtown living because of the proximity to various "parlor houses" he frequented and the lovely *filles de joie* who provided him company. When the madame of a bordello at Eighth and York became pregnant, a significant problem developed, when she accused Alfred DuPont himself of being the father. The woman, Maggie Payne, confronted Alfred DuPont at his Galt House suites, but he refused to accept any responsibility and sent her away. When she pleaded with him to acknowledge the child or help pay for its upbringing, he refused again, and she – so the story goes – shot him straight through the heart.

A scandal of this magnitude would have rocked the DuPont family in modern times, so one can imagine the uproar it would have produced in the image-conscious Victorian society of *fin-de-siècle* Louisville,

Kentucky. After a hurried family conference, one of Uncle Fr nephews, Thomas Coleman DuPont, smuggled the body back Wilmington under cover of darkness, and after a few pay-offs, the police backed the heart-attack story, and the newspapers published a fictitious account of the death. (The fact that the editor of the Louisville paper was heavily in debt to Mr. DuPont might have played a part here.) Maggie Payne was never prosecuted, and DuPont family members managed to keep the truth behind Alfred's death hidden – at least locally – well into the 1930s when they finally started to reluctantly acknowledge the details of the scandal. Two days after the death was announced in Louisville papers, the *Cincinnati Enquirer* ran a story revealing all the sordid details, but many Old Louisvillians conveniently chose not to accept that account of the story.

Alfred's brother Biderman continued to live in the country villa for several more years after the scandal, although he eventually returned to the family estate in Delaware, where he died in 1904. His seven children still had use of the estate after his departure, and DuPont Square still hosted many special events that drew large crowds of Louisvillians to its front lawn. After Biderman DuPont's death, the city carried out its plans to use the grounds for a public park, and hired the famed Olmsted Brothers to do the design. Not too long thereafter reports of a strange caped figure allegedly began to surface. Many people assumed it to be the ghost of Biderman DuPont himself, since he had loved his country estate so much and could often be seen strolling the grounds after dark. However, when details of the scandal surfaced some thirty years later, rumors started to circulate that Uncle Fred had returned from the grave to clear his name, even though it seemed that public sentiment clearly weighed in on the side of Maggie Payne.

Clancy Berger recalls many summer evenings when he and his brother would play stickball in Central Park, very often long into the night after darkness had fallen and his mother had sent their sister out to fetch them home. He remembers an eerie encounter on one occasion as he ran to retrieve a ball lost in the grass: "I had just stooped under a tree where I thought I would find the ball, when I noticed a strange figure approaching me. He was wearing a cape and big hat, but I couldn't make out much else because the light was behind him. And I remember that it must have been late summer, because you could feel a bit of the

air. And it was sort of humid and damp all around,
usual fog rising from the earth." As the young boy
man supposedly stopped and held out his hand.
ball I was looking for! He just sort of half tossed
it rolled to my feet, and then he was gone! *Like he hadn't
even been there at all.* The fog was pretty thick then, so I figure he disappeared into it. When I asked my friends about it, they said it was the ghost of Uncle Fred looking for his illegitimate son."

Others have claimed to see a shadowy caped figure in the park after dark as well, and some old-timers refer to it as the 'Ghost of Uncle Fred.' Although the apparition doesn't appear to frighten anyone, an encounter with Uncle Fred can be quite unsettling. When darkness falls over old DuPont Square, and a faint wind gently rustles the leaves overhead, some even claim they have heard the music of an organ grinder off in the distance, and on lazy summer evenings the happy voices of visitors from a forgotten time can be heard lilting in the air.

MORE ABOUT THE
SOUTHERN EXPOSITION

Central Park's former life is inextricably linked to the world-famous Southern Exposition of 1883, a would-be world's fair of its day that put Louisville on the map and led to the development of today's Old Louisville neighborhood. Although the Derby City had entertained the notion of hosting a large exposition since the end of the Civil War, it began to seriously consider holding its own grand Southern Exposition after the successful Atlanta Cotton Expo of 1881. Biderman DuPont himself served as chairman of the expo committee, and many feel that this directly influenced his choice of the exposition location on the site of the present-day Saint James Court, and just steps from the family estate in DuPont Square. Although the Louisville city limits at that time had reached to within several blocks of today's Central Park, locals still considered the area south of the park "wilderness." Laborers spent months draining the swamps and clearing land, and before long a mag-

THE GREAT SOUTHERN EXPOSITION
THROWS ITS DOORS OPEN TO THE WORLD.

A VIEW OF THE MAGNIFICENT BUILDING.

A PLAN OF THE GROUND FLOOR,
Showing Accurately the Location of All the Various Departments, the Machinery, the Annex, the Farm, the Flower Garden, I

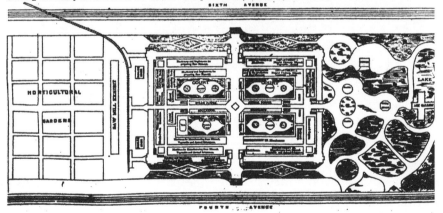

The grand Southern Exposition in Louisville, Kentucky was essentially the World Fair of the time. Opened in 1883 by President Chester A. Arthur, it ran annually for five years, proclaiming the rebirth of Southern industry, and highlighting the innovations of the day. Thomas Edison personally turned on the switch to light the Exposition with the largest display of electric lighting outside of New York, and the electric trolley car premiered here, riding delighted passengers through lighted tunnels.

nificent exposition building – reputedly the largest wooden structure in the world – covered the thirteen acres of land.

The Southern Exposition with the theme "From Seed to Loom" opened amid much fanfare on August 1, 1883, with President Chester A. Arthur presiding and Thomas Edison supervising the first throw of the switch. Central Park became both midway and entrance to the fair, and almost 5,000 incandescent electric light bulbs illuminated the building and grounds, the largest concentration of the newfangled electric lights anywhere at that time, even more than in New York City. For this reason Old Louisville bragged for many years that it was one of the earliest neighborhoods lit by electricity in the nation.

Melville O. Briney nostalgically captured the feeling experienced by many visitors to the exposition in one of her many *Fond Recollection* articles from the late 1940s and '50s in the *Louisville Times*: "Ask anyone who was a child back in the '80s and he will tell you about that breathtaking experience. For no matter how often he saw it (and families went over and over again), the miracle was always the same." She wrote, "There was a quiet that covered the waiting crowds. Then an amber glow began to seep through the dusk, brightening, brightening – until what had been familiar corridors of the big barn-like building became for him aisles of blinding light and beauty, touched with the gold of heaven."

A reporter commented: "Mr. Edison's fabulous display of 4,800 incandescent lights of 16-candle power each comes on every evening to bedazzle the beholder. The contract with the Edison Company is the largest ever made for lighting a building with electric lights. The cost of the plant was $100,000 alone, and it is said to have taken 100 men working constantly for a month to string all the wires and to get the equipment in working order..." Given the attention Mr. Edison received during his time in Louisville, does it come as any surprise that several residents of Saint James Court claim that his spirit still walks the grounds that he illuminated in such a revolutionary fashion so many years ago? A young couple left its Belgravia Court townhouse in the early 1990s for an afternoon stroll and claims a "gentleman who looked just like Thomas Edison materialized out of nowhere, looked around as if lost, and then vanished." Perhaps his spirit has returned to check on the progress made since then.

Not surprisingly, the Southern Exposition was a phenomenal

success, and hundreds of thousands of visitors showed up in the first season alone. Originally scheduled to last for only three months, the "expo" ended up closing four years later in 1887. For many, these would be the golden years for Central Park, a time when it served more as an amusement park than the quiet oasis it is today. A roller coaster, still a recent invention, joined the park grounds, and a racetrack hosted some of Louisville's earliest bicycle races. Laborers constructed a large bandstand, and some of the nation's leading bands and orchestras gave frequent concerts.

Park officials also had a man-made paddleboat lake installed and a fireproof art museum as well, where paintings and other works of art from the collections of J.P. Morgan, John Jacob Astor, Jay Gould, and the Smithsonian Institution – among others – could be viewed. An electric railway, designed by Edison, took visitors around the exposition grounds and all around Central Park. A few years later Louisville would have one of the best electric trolley systems in the country, and at least twice as many street railroads as any other city its size.

Central Park still attracted large crowds even after the closing of the Southern Exposition; however, it soon became apparent that the enormous Southern Exposition building would not be needed for long. Workers gradually dismantled the buildings and used many of the materials in other local construction projects such as the infirmary building still standing at 1412 South Sixth Street and the Fireworks Amphitheater & Auditorium that once stood at the southwest corner of Fourth and Hill Streets. Developers took over the expo grounds and formed the Victoria Land Company, deciding to go with an aristocratic-London-inspired theme. Centered around an elegant mall of landscaped green spaces and an impressive fountain, the streets would be named Saint James Court, Belgravia Court, Fountain Court and Victoria Place (now Magnolia). An added feature would be the unique "walking courts" that added some extra green space and seclusion to an already tranquil neighborhood. As a result, the park-like layout of Saint James Court merged with the green space of Central Park, turning the whole area into one of the most desirable residential districts in the city. Before long, it would be home to Louisville's economic and intellectual elite, a favored spot for business magnates and a number of artists, writers, musicians, poets and architects as well.

A small stone marker at the entrance to Saint James Court com-memorates the Southern Exposition, and just steps from that, the love-ly Conrad-Caldwell House towers over sidewalks that trace the paths of visitors from a hundred and twenty years ago. Even if recycled materials from the huge exhibit hall can be found throughout Old Louisville, not much else remains from the grand Southern Exposition of 1883, other than newspaper clippings, stories and memories. Every night, just before night falls, the gas lanterns that line the walking courts and grassy boule-vard of Louisville's most prestigious neighborhood click on with a hiss and bathe the area in a soft, nostalgic glow. Although the electric lights that debuted here so long ago still remain, gaslight has always been the preferred choice on Saint James Court.

Chapter 6

FOUNTAIN COURT

At the center of the boulevard that runs the length of Saint James Court, and well within view of the Conrad-Caldwell House, a large fountain splashes day and night. Locals consider this the center of Saint James Court, and as such, the heart of Old Louisville. It is reputedly the most romantic spot in the city, and on warm summer nights when couples, hand in hand, stroll by its cascading, shimmering waters bathed in the soft glow of the gas light, you can see why. The romantic, nostalgic feel of this fountain is eternal, and it sparks the same tender feelings in many throughout the entire year. Some enjoy it most in the spring among the explosive displays of magnolia and dogwood blossoms; others cannot wait for the fall months to arrive so they can treat themselves to a late-October afternoon spent kicking around in the golden leaves that have rained down through the chilly air. There are even those who prefer to see the icy fingers of winter at work on the fountain, content to behold a frozen and silent mass of sculpted metal and snow on a bleak January morning. Just like the seasons, the fountain only adds to the charm of Saint James Court.

To the east of the fountain, a strip of green known as Fountain Court cuts a short path to the elegant mansions of Fourth Street, another thoroughfare famed for its impressive collection of homes. Tranquil and serene, the shady lawns of Fountain Court offer a bit of oasis for those in search of peace and quiet. But if you're tempted to visit the calm green spaces of Fountain Court, be forewarned that you might not be the only one there in search of peace and solace. One of Old Louisville's most famed ghosts, *the Widow Hoag*, lurks in the shadows while time slowly passes, waiting for the return of a lost child who will never come home.

The story of the Widow Hoag, as she has come to be known, is a well-known one in the neighborhood, and it has been told since the 1940s, the period that marked the beginning of the decline of Old Louisville. By this time, many families couldn't afford to keep such large homes, and owners converted many of the huge mansions and residences in the area into apartments and rooming houses. The widowed Mrs. Hoag lived in a third-floor apartment on Fountain Court during World War II, and when the Air Force sent away her only son to fight in the Pacific, it devastated her.

Neighbors remember the day military representatives arrived with the news that Mrs. Hoag's son had died a terrible death trying to land his plane on an aircraft carrier. "It was so tragic," says one of them. "They never found the body, so Mrs. Hoag refused to believe he was dead. She was sure he'd come home someday, so she insisted she would have to stay there so he could find her." The distraught woman became a recluse, but she stayed on in the apartment and waited for her lost son, believing until the day she died that he would return to her. Most of the neighbors have moved away, but many believe the spirit of the Widow Hoag never left Fountain Court, even though they carried her body away years ago.

"The house is still there, and I'm sure the widow is still there, too." Nora Jackson lived on Fountain Court in the 1970s and claims she had several odd encounters with the Widow Hoag when she lived in an apartment that faced the building where the Hoags rented their third floor rooms. Although she hasn't been back to the Louisville area in over fifteen years, the former librarian says Old Louisville holds a special place in heart, despite the scare she got while living on Fountain Court. "Spirits remain earthbound because they haven't accepted their own death or the death of a loved one," she explains, "and I think that must

Fountain Court, one of Old Louisville's famed walking courts and home to the Widow Hoag, its most famous ghost.

have been the case with Mrs. Hoag. She probably doesn't even realize she's passed and is still waiting for her son to come home from the war."

A part-time student at Jefferson Community College, Jackson had heard several stories about the Widow Hoag before she moved to Fountain Court from her Fifth Street apartment, but she never expected to have one of her own to tell one day. "I lived in the house across the green from the house she and her son had lived in," Nora explains, "and my boyfriend at the time lived on the other end of the court. He's the one who had told me the stories about her in the first place." Jackson says both she and her boyfriend spent a lot of time chatting and smoking in the grassy area in front of their respective apartments. "One night, right around Halloween, we decided to go to a movie downtown, so as we're walking toward the Fourth Street gate, this weird shape comes out of the shadows of the house right towards us!" recalls Nora. "It was an old woman, all dressed in black! And it was like she was floating along the ground. She didn't have feet or anything that I could see!" Her boyfriend had just recounted a story about an alleged ghost at the old seminary building at the college, and because of this, she claims "the apparition was especially freaky." She assumed it had to be a practical joke.

But the startled girl watched as the shadowy apparition approached her boyfriend and passed through him before vanishing on the other side of the green, leaving only an icy draft in her wake. "You know who that was, don't you?" The boyfriend enquired. "I said it had to be the Widow Hoag," she responded. "It's Mrs. Hoag and she thought you were her lost son finally coming back home."

Not too long after that, a family moved into the actual renovated apartment where Mrs. Hoag had lived, and they, too, would soon witness an apparition from another time and place. The teenage son had just returned from a party at a friend's house, and found himself all alone in the apartment. This didn't bother him until he witnessed the figure of an old woman in black who glided across the floor and disappeared into a solid wall. "It scared the pants off of me!" he confesses, "and I ran outside and didn't go back inside until my parents got home. When I told them what happened, they didn't believe me, but not too long afterwards, somebody told my mother that the Widow Hoag had lived in that very same apartment." The man, who now lives in California, says he saw the shadowy form on several occasions after that. "I finally got so I wasn't scared of her," he explains. "Someone told me about her son getting killed at sea, and his body never coming back home, so I understood where she was coming from and I actually felt sorry for her. All she wants is a little peace."

Perhaps the Widow Hoag will get some peace one of these days. A local psychic claims she can find this peace by locating the spirit of her lost son. It seems, according to this woman, who lives just steps from Fountain Court, that the world abounds with restless spirits and other lost souls in search of loved ones and familiar ground. She's certain that it is just a matter of time before the son who died so many years ago finds his mother and gives her the reassurance she's been longing for. Until then, her saddened spirit will have to lurk in the shadows of quiet Fountain Court, sharing the cool, grassy spaces with the living while life goes on.

ABOUT THE
LEGEND OF THE ICE BOY

On a bitterly cold day in the winter of 1912, half of Louisville turned out to behold a spectacular sight at the Saint James Court entrance to Fountain Court. Looming before the onlookers, an eerie vision in ice and snow towered five stories overhead, the remnants of a terrible fire from the night before. The Saint James Apartments – otherwise known as "Conrad's Folly" because of Theopholis Conrad's insistence on constructing a then-unheard-of-five-story apartment building – had caught fire, totally destroying the top two floors. As firemen battled the blaze in the frigid night air, water cascaded down the sides of the building and froze in place, leaving behind a magnificent sculpture of stalagmites and crystallized ash. The three bottom stories still stand today, and although no one perished in the calamity, older residents of Saint James Court still talk about the 'Legend of the Ice Boy.'

Rumor has it that a young boy from the nearby Cabbage Patch district – not wanting to return to the freezing temperatures outside – had supposedly fallen asleep on the top floor of the building after running an errand there. Although it was never substantiated, rumor claimed he died in the fire, and his ghost can still be seen wandering around Saint James Court in the wintertime.

Chapter 7

THE HOME OF LADY ROSS

Old Louisville, like much of Kentucky, has become aware of the many negative stereotypes surrounding the state. Ever since East Coast reporters unfairly – and incorrectly – portrayed Kentuckians as little more than backwoods savages while national attention focused on the notorious feud between the Hatfields and McCoys in the 1890s, it seems that the Bluegrass has had to fight an uphill battle to maintain its good name. However, in true southern fashion, Old Louisvillians don't lend much credence to outsiders' opinions, as long as they're free to enjoy the generous slice of gentility they cut for themselves over a hundred years ago. A tumbler of mellow bourbon in hand, many of us sit in our front parlors, surrounded by damask draperies and green velvet cushions, hardwood oak floors inlaid with cherry and walnut, patisseried ceilings, crystal chandeliers and elegant fireplaces, while we thumb our noses through large stained-glass windows at would-be encroachers who don't love our neighborhood as much as we do. Isolation, we tell ourselves, is a small price to pay for refinement that money can't buy.

After all, as any Old Louisvillian will tell you, *this* was the first neighborhood in the nation to make widespread use of electric lights, and for decades it enjoyed one of the best public transit systems around. In addition, no residential neighborhood in the country could boast the high number of comfortable, elegant homes or the same impressive standard of living that characterized day-to-day existence in Old Louisville. A *Courier-Journal* reporter touted these virtues in an article from September, 1888, saying, "As a residence city...Louisville enjoys many remarkable advantages, not the least of which is the taste which has been characteristic, from the first, in the beautifying of and building of homes." People in the 1800s even talked about how well inhabitants of Louisville ate, compared to other cities across the country. By the time the city had barely completed its second decade of existence, the state's thriving commercial wineries – the largest in the nation – provided a steady and generous supply of fine wines to local dinner tables. Old Louisvillians, as a consequence, have always prided themselves on their homes and knowing how to live well.

"The stranger within our gates has ever remarked that Louisville homes far outclass those of other cities," proclaimed the *Louisville Times* in 1909, commenting on an astounding two-decade explosion in local home construction. This sense of residential well-being and contentment caught the attention of more than one visitor to Louisville. Famed director Walter Damrosch, for example, made the following observation after he brought the New York Symphony Orchestra to delight Louisville audiences during two seasons of the Southern Exposition in 1885 and 1886: "I shall always look back on those two summers with delight and gratitude...Louisville at that time was a small community, but with an old civilization which manifested itself in a circle of charming people of established culture and social relations."

It's little wonder, then, in a time when a man's home was his castle, that Old Louisvillians felt somewhat like royalty. During the Gilded Age, residents of Old Louisville, like most of wealthy Victorian America, paid extra special attention to taste and good manners. And true to fashion, they were obsessed with all things noble and aristocratic. In 1895, the country was titillated when *two* American heiresses bagged royal husbands from European nobility. For weeks, newspapers ran accounts of the courtships and marriages of Consuelo Vanderbilt to Charles Richard John Spencer Churchill, ninth Duke of Marlborough, and Anna Gould to Count Paul Ernest Boniface de Castellane.

This unassuming residence at 1438 South Fourth Street was once the setting for a royal wedding. A haunting apparition of the unhappy bride is said to appear every November, the month an Old Louisville girl married a Scottish baronet in 1901.

In 1901 Louisville buzzed with the news that one of its own would join the ranks of European nobility. In a quiet ceremony at 1438 South Fourth Street, Patty Burnley Ellison married Sir Charles Henry Augustus Lockhart Ross, ninth Baronet of Balnagown. Patty, the daughter of an Old Louisville family of modest means, had met and fallen in love with Sir Charles on an Atlantic crossing. After the exchange of the marriage vows in Louisville, the couple traveled to Scotland, where a wedding party was held at Balnagown Castle, part of Sir Charles' family's estate since 1672. Given the storybook circumstances surrounding the engagement, most of Old Louisville assumed the marriage would be a happy one – especially since this seemed to be a marriage for love, – unlike the marriages of Anna Gould and Consuelo Vanderbilt. Whereas both the heiresses who had married to obtain royal titles came from the wealthiest families in the USA, Patty Burnley Ellison came from a modest family. Patty had the added good fortune that her husband counted as the largest landowner in the British Isles. By all accounts, they were to have a life of wedded bliss.

However, within several years, the new Lady Ross realized hers would not be a happy marriage. True, she had the advantage of living a life of luxury in Europe; nonetheless, she could not count a faithful husband as one of her gains. Although she remained married to Sir Charles Ross for many years, her life was full of sadness. Since she left the family home on Fourth Street over a hundred years ago, some believe her spirit has returned to search out the happiness she once knew there. Several prior residents of the house at 1438 South Fourth Street claim they have seen the apparition of an elegant woman in attire from the Edwardian era, the period when Lady Ross first realized she would not have a happy life. On several occasions people have sighted a spectral form with pearls around her neck, sadly making her way down the very same stairs she used to make her wedding-day entrance over a hundred years ago.

Sandy Carter had told the story about "the regal-looking woman on the stairs" she had seen many times before she discovered that the former Lady Ross had lived in the house where she rented an apartment over ten years ago. "The first time I saw her was right before Thanksgiving, and it had just snowed outside," she recalls. "I got up early one morning, before the sun had even come up, and while I was in the kitchen I saw this woman walking by the stairs, just a plain as the nose on your face." Sandy remembers that the woman had a "matronly, kind appearance, and she was very well-kempt." Carter, a single mother of two at the time, claims the woman's elegant bearing struck her as out of the ordinary. "I thought to myself that it must have been someone from the '20s or '30s, since she was so classy and was wearing that kind of stuff...Then I realized I had to be seeing a ghost of someone who lived there." As soon as the apparition appeared, Carter says it vanished. Although she remembers seeing the same apparition on several different occasions, Sandy claims she never felt frightened or experienced apprehension.

Several other former residents of the house at 1438 South Fourth Street claim they have witnessed the same apparition, and like Sandy Carter, it didn't appear to bother any of them. They also made special note of the fact that "she looked like a real lady" and sensed an air of sadness about her. Lady Ross finally divorced her husband in 1928, and when she died on February 5, 1947, she had become a bit of a local icon. Although she never returned to her hometown, other than for happy visits, she served as a sort of correspondent for a local paper, commenting in her columns on British politics and society. On one occasion, a former acquaintance of Lady Ross claims to have seen her apparition in his offices at the *Courier-Journal*. He, like the others, reported no fear at the encounter, "only a tinge of sadness and bit of admiration for the courageous lady who was dressed to the nines." Oddly enough, all these occurrences seem to happen in November, the month when Patty Ellison wed Sir Charles in her family's Fourth Street residence.

ABOUT THE BRENNAN HOUSE

In the late 1800s, when young Patty Ellison enjoyed her privileged, albeit modest, upbringing in the family home on Fourth Street, horse-drawn carriages and buggies clip-clopped their way around downtown Louisville. Nearby Macauley's Theater on Walnut played host to some of the country's finest artists, and Jennie Benedict's famous afternoon teas set the stage for an impressive display of local fashion and social etiquette. In the Louisville of the 19th century, scores of homes reflecting the grace and ease of the Victorian era lined Fifth Street north of Broadway. Today, the center of the Derby City has undergone a drastic change, and very little remains to hint at the original character of old-time Louisville. However, just outside the boundaries of the Old Louisville neighborhood and only blocks away from towering skyscrapers, a solitary house still stands. Listed on the National Register of Historic Places, locals know it as the Brennan House, and it has survived virtually untouched, an authentic keepsake from a bygone era.

Like so many Victorian homes in Louisville, the Brennan House drew on the best local craftsmen and artisans for its solid brick-and-mortar construction. Fairly typical for its time, the three-story façade has been painted chocolate brown with trim accents. Inside, elaborate crystal and etched-glass chandeliers cast a soft glow on highly-polished hardwood floors and rich wood trim. Light fixtures dually compatible for gas and electric power can be seen, and in the parlor, two original calla lily design gas lamps protrude from the walls and bathe the sophisticated interior in a warm glow. Throughout the house, flawless woodwork, rich wall coverings and furnishings abound. Stained-glass coats-of-arms by Louisville artist Bernard Alberts, massive hand-carved dining room and bedroom furniture, and a signed Tiffany lamp offer just a taste of the opulent appointments enjoyed by the Brennan family.

Although the Italianate masterpiece dates from 1868, when a local distiller had it built, Thomas Brennan moved into the six-bedroom house with his wife, Anna Bruce, in 1884. The house bears their name today because they occupied it for almost ninety years before bequeathing it to the Filson Club Historical Society. Brennan, a native of Ireland and a prominent inventor, had nine children with his wife. Eight of the children survived into adulthood and grew up in the house and enjoyed an extremely close-knit family life. The family home always served as the center of activity for the Brennans, but they also mingled with Louisville society and traveled extensively. It was rumored, in fact, that hardly a time passed when some member of the family couldn't be found in Europe. They displayed souvenirs of their trips all through the house, and visitors can view many family heirlooms from furniture to artwork to knickknacks.

*A true Victorian time capsule, the Brennan House still survives in
downtown Louisville.*

Tour the lovely home, and a well-informed guide will explain
that although the Brennan family enjoyed no local or national renown
while alive, they do now for the collections they left behind. Entirely
original to the Brennan family, the contents of the Brennan House range

from the death masks of Thomas and Anna Brennan to linens and perfume bottles, and china and stemware. Other treasures include an ornate silver service, a collection of family portraits, a library containing richly-bound volumes and various steamer trunks containing memorabilia of world travels. As the staff likes to point out, "Very few homes in the entire country can boast such an original collection." The mansion is entirely furnished with original Brennan belongings, and the visitor experiences a true visit to the past. For this reason, many have called the Brennan House a veritable time capsule.

The *Courier-Journal* has described the Brennan House as "an echo of what Fifth Street once was, a choice residential neighborhood on the edge of downtown," and each year thousands of visitors enjoy the elegance of this bygone era. Over the years, however, people have come to suspect that the Brennans left behind more than just many of their personal belongings at 631 South Fifth Street. The mansion is said to house several restless spirits. Many speculate as to their identities, but most agree that much of the activity involves the ghost of the one Brennan child who did not survive childhood in the house. A volunteer at the house has seen a baby crib rocking wildly by itself, and others have heard the faint sobs of a child on various occasions. The smell of cigar smoke often pervades the "smoke free" study, and blurs of white light have been spotted flashing across the second-floor hallway.

Jonas Whitliff served as volunteer tour guide at the Fifth Street mansion for a year while he completed his studies at nearby Spalding University. "I had heard that there were ghosts in the old townhouse, but I never expected to witness anything myself," he explains. "One afternoon, I was there alone, though, and it got really creepy for a while. It was late afternoon in October and it was dark out already. The wind was howling outside, and the leaves were dancing in the icy wind." Jonas says his job that afternoon required some light cleaning work before he checked in with the director and left for his dorm room. "I finished my tidying up, and was coming down the front stair so I could put the cleaning bucket and cleanser back in the closet. Down in the entry hall, I noticed a shape there, and it struck me as odd. *Was it a person?* I couldn't tell at first."

The twenty-year old student of English literature claims a milky form materialized in front of him and appeared to hover a foot off the floor. What seemed like hours passed, but he figures it couldn't have been more than a minute before he discerned the outline of a man and some vague facial features to the form. "It was all in whites and grays, so it was hard to make things out. But it looked like a man from the 1880s to me," Jonas recalls, adding that "I was able to smell the smoke of a cigar, too. It was very obvious." In another minute or two, he says, the form started to fade and then became invisible. "It was definitely creepy! I went and told the director what had happened and she just laughed a bit. I guess she had gotten used to people telling her things like that."

Jonas doesn't volunteer at the elegant Brennan mansion on Fifth Street anymore, but he says he does stop in for a visit at least two or three times a year. Every time he does, he claims he gets "the faint whiff of cigar smoke" and on one occasion he swears he caught a glimpse of something blurry speed by the mirror, "even though there was nobody near the mirror." Jonas recommends you come to the Brennan House with an open mind and enjoy the treasures from the past that are on display there. If you're lucky, you might get a real glimpse of the past.

Chapter 8

J.B. SPEED ART MUSEUM

L ocated on the northern fringes of the University of Louisville campus, the J.B. Speed Art Museum is Kentucky's oldest and largest art museum, with over 12,000 pieces in its holdings. The extensive collection spans 6,000 years and ranges from ancient Egyptian to contemporary art, and the galleries include seventeenth-century Dutch and Flemish paintings, eighteenth-century French art, Renaissance and Baroque tapestries, and significant pieces of contemporary American painting and sculpture as well. The Speed also houses portraits, sculpture, furniture, and decorative arts by Kentucky artists and other noted works created specifically for Kentuckians. Designed by Louisville architect Arthur Loomis in the Greek Revival style, the beautiful limestone building at 2035 South Third Street opened its doors on January 15, 1927 and since then has become an important fixture on the Old Louisville social scene. In addition to numerous collections of art, the Speed Art Museum also houses at least one ghost.

Theories abound as to who - *or what* - might be haunting the Speed Art Museum; however, one commonly held notion is that Harriet "Hattie" Bishop Speed, the wife of the museum's namesake, still walks the galleries of the institution she founded in 1925 as a memorial to her

One alleged haunt of this Old Louisville landmark is none other that the benefactress herself, Miss Hattie Speed, who founded it as a memorial to her late husband, J.B. Speed.

late husband, James Breckinridge Speed, a prominent Louisville businessman and philanthropist. An accomplished concert pianist in her own right, Hattie Bishop Speed championed music and the arts in Louisville and for years provided a music room in her own Old Louisville mansion for community recitals and concerts by the local Bach Club. When she died in 1942, leaving behind a legacy as Old Louisville's premier patron of the arts, Hattie Bishop Speed had established herself as a pillar in the neighborhood and across the state. By all accounts, she was an upstanding citizen who was devoted to her husband. An inscription added to the front of the building after her death reads: "*The world is a nobler place that she passed this way.*" However, Hattie Bishop Speed might have suffered from at least one minor flaw: Jealousy.

Many people who have researched the strange goings-on at the Speed Art Museum feel that the unexplained antics suggest those of a jealous wife, most likely Harriet "Hattie" Bishop herself. Although she spent six years happily married to James Breckinridge Speed, when he died in 1912, Hattie felt more than just sadness at his passing. She had been Mr. Speed's second wife, and as such, feelings of rivalry and inadequacy sometimes plagued her. Cora A. Coffin of Cincinnati, the *first* Mrs. Speed, had borne him two children, and after her death, she left a large void in his life. In 1925, Hattie Bishop Speed founded the museum and dedicated it as a memorial to her beloved husband in 1927, perhaps as a way of outdoing Mr. Speed's first wife.

Wanda Nichols worked at the J.B. Speed Art Museum in Louisville for many years, and although she has no personal accounts of the ghost herself, she has heard many first-hand accounts told by other employees there. Motion sensors seem to go off without explanation, for example, and odd wisps of something white and diaphanous have been reported on video monitors. According to Nichols, the museum staff believes that there may actually be two ghosts, but no one can say for sure. Generally, however, most employees believe that a main ghost haunts the premises – that of Hattie Bishop Speed, founder of the museum. Wanda says, "You can tell when Miss Hattie is around because you can smell the faint rose-type perfume that she used to wear. I've smelled that perfume myself, but only in one room: Gallery 3, the nineteenth-century art collection." Interestingly enough, Miss Hattie and her husband purchased many of the paintings in that gallery themselves while on some of their many trips abroad.

Perhaps the most startling story about Miss Hattie that Ms. Nichols has heard concerns the night something unexplained triggered the museum alarm system. She recalls, "Before the present security measures were put into place, the museum contracted its security out to an alarm company which was notified electronically whenever an alarm was tripped. An alarm went off one night in the late 1990s, and the company came out with a guard dog to search the museum." Nichols says that when the guard dog entered Gallery 2, the area for eighteenth-century art, it looked up into the northwest corner of the room near the ceiling and froze. Something suddenly frightened it, and it broke loose from its handlers and ran to another section of the museum, where it cowered in a corner until it could finally be coaxed away. "No one knows what frightened it," she says, "but presumably it was the ghost of Miss Hattie, perhaps upset that a dog would be allowed in the museum."

Another frequently-heard story concerns a security guard who had fallen asleep downstairs in the Native American gallery, a basement area notorious for its many odd occurrences. The guard suddenly awoke to see, standing over him, the ghost of a woman in a white dress, an apparition that has been spotted on various occasions. Nichols explains, "Some visitors to the museum report feeling a bit spooked when they're in that area, for no real reason. At night when they're alone, the security guards at the museum say that sometimes they can spot an ethereal form traveling through some of the galleries at the museum. Presumably it's Miss Hattie, making sure that everything is all right."

On another occasion two security guards took the elevator down to the lowest level of the museum, and reportedly had an unsettling encounter when the elevator doors opened. Standing in the hallway, the apparition of a woman in white greeted them and then disappeared, leaving them in stunned silence. The hallway leads to the Native American gallery.

Nichols also adds as a side note that the elevators themselves have been the focal point of other strange events, and not just possible sightings of Miss Hattie. "On occasion, certain elevators will start up when no one has punched a button to go from floor to floor," she explains. There also seem to be occasional problems with the freight elevator at the rear of the building. For no apparent reason at all, the doors will close all by themselves, and then the car will travel up or down to the next floor. "It seems to happen only at night, not during working hours," comments Wanda. "This problem has been investigated by professionals, and they have told the museum it's a hydraulic problem, that sometimes the elevator needs to adjust its hydraulic pressure. I don't know anything about this, and perhaps that's true of all hydraulic lifts," she says. "Those professionals may be correct, but I've always thought it rather spooky. It also seems odd that it happens only at night."

It has been said that Hattie Bishop Speed rather acted the part of the perfectionist and spent many hours in the museum, checking progress and making sure her orders were followed to the letter, oftentimes into the late hours of the night, and sometimes by herself. Does

Miss Hattie still continue her nightly visits to check on the progress of the museum she founded over seventy-five years ago?

A strange occurrence that suggests a jealous woman might be afoot took place in 2001 when one of the employees responsible for maintaining the information plaques for the works of art noticed that one of the labels for a painting in Gallery 4, the Kentucky Room, kept peeling off the wall and falling to the floor. She would put more and more adhesive on the back of the label, yet later it would still be found lying on the floor. According to Nichols, the label identifies a portrait of the first Mrs. Speed, Cora Coffin. "Is Miss Hattie upset that her painting is hanging in the gallery?" she wonders. "There are no portraits of Miss Hattie. The employee replaced the label altogether with a new one, and it hasn't peeled off yet; however, the label for another painting then started lifting off the wall." This picture featured an attractive gypsy girl who lived in Louisville around the turn of the last century, when Miss Hattie was still alive, and Mr. Speed was supposedly heard on several occasions to make favorable remarks about the gypsy woman's beauty. "It's possible that these labels just aren't being given enough adhesive initially; then again, these are the only two labels we seem to have problems with," explains Wanda Nichols. Could it be possible that Hattie Speed had a jealous streak that survived over into this life?

Julia Simpson, a mother of four and lifetime resident of Old Louisville, thinks this is probably the case. The former employee at the J.B. Speed Art Museum remembers several experiences – all of them in the Kentucky Room – that made her suspect that Miss Hattie might have a jealous streak. That is, if indeed the ghost of the benefactress still walks the marbled halls of the institution. For years Simpson hasn't told a single person about the strange things she witnessed in the Speed Museum, afraid that friends and colleagues would ridicule her, but for this book she decided to share her story.

"One evening," she recalls, "I found myself alone in the Kentucky Room doing some tidying up and arranging for an event the next day. It must have been around 9:00, and I was almost ready to finish up and go home. I was walking past the portrait of the first Mrs. Speed, and I noticed that it wasn't hanging quite right on the wall, so I went and straightened it before getting back to business." About five minutes passed, and Julia prepared herself to leave. However, she wasn't prepared to see what she saw as she walked past the portrait again. "There, on the floor, was the painting!" she explains. "It was standing up against the wall, like someone had taken it down and set it there. And it had been turned around so the image of Mrs. Speed was facing the wall!" She quickly left, the portrait still on the floor, and decided to let someone worry about rehanging it the next morning.

Several weeks later Julia Simpson found herself again in the same part of the museum. Although she had already heard many accounts of strange happenings in the Speed by this time, she decided it would be better to remain silent about the incident with the portrait of Mrs. Speed, and for this reason no one had any reason to suspect that she might feel uneasy in Gallery 4. But this is exactly how she felt as she busied herself that night with the cataloging of various items by noted Kentucky artists. "I had been keeping a nervous eye on the portrait of Mrs. Speed the whole evening," she recalls, "hoping it wouldn't start levitating off the wall or anything, so I wasn't really paying attention to the other parts of the gallery."

Julia turned around to face the wall opposite the one where the portrait of Mrs. Speed hung, and noticed what appeared to be a thin, white strip of fog floating across the room. "I saw this misty, wispy thing in the air, about half way between the floor and the ceiling, and I knew it wasn't fog right away. I could actually see it move and slightly change form, and it shimmered and sort of gave off a weird, yellowish glow." Aware that the temperature about her had suddenly dropped, the trembling woman watched for several minutes as the strange mist slowly rose and concentrated itself in the corner of the room. Although it never seemed to take on a recognizable form, the diaphanous, white shape elongated itself several times and thinned out before contracting back to its original size.

"It was moving almost like a cloud would," Julia explains, "slowly and steadily, so slow in fact that you didn't notice it was moving at first. And you could also see the shape of the thing changing and moving, but it wasn't a cloud at all. It was hard to determine the actual perimeter of the shape because it seemed that it just slowly dissolved and became invisible." According to the rest of her description, the strange mass seemed denser in the center and less dense, almost transparent, around the edges, and by the time it had risen to the ceiling, she noticed that a small glowing orb hovered near it. "It was a small, golden sphere that moved independently of the wisp or whatever it was, and I don't know how long it had been there before I noticed it. It could have been there the whole time, for all I know." Julia Simpson watched for another minute or two, and then she claims the strange strip of fog just slowly faded and became invisible.

"I think ghosts and all that stuff is a bunch of bunk," she confesses, "so I wouldn't say I saw a ghost or anything. However, it *was* extremely weird and unnerving. Definitely unexplainable...I don't know what it was, just like I don't know how the picture got off the wall that time." Julia quickly left the gallery after the misty form evaporated and when she returned to work the next day, she kept her skepticism – and her story as well – to herself. Three days later she would have a final and most unnerving encounter in the same gallery.

Once again, the museum had closed, and something required Julia's attention in the Kentucky Gallery. Except for two custodians on the other side of the building, she was alone. "I had just gone through a file, and I was holding it in my hand as I turned to go to another gallery, when all of a sudden I felt something brush past me," she says. "I couldn't see anything at all, but it felt just like a person had walked in front of me and almost pushed me out of the way. The room got really cold, and you could smell the very faint scent of roses or maybe rose water. It might have been the perfume Miss Hattie supposedly wore all the time," explains Julia Simpson, "but I don't know. It was a smell I had never quite smelled before." When she looked down at the file in her hand, Julia realized that it had vanished.

"I spent almost an hour searching for it hour before I finally found it...down in the Native American gallery!" she recalls. "And when I finally did find it, I smelled the same rose perfume I had smelled in the other gallery. I got a very eerie feeling from then on whenever I went into the Kentucky Room, especially when I was around the portrait of Mrs. Speed." Ms. Simpson, however, only worked another month or thereabouts at the Speed Museum before she quit to take another job at a different museum. Although she claims her experiences with unexplained phenomena in the museum had nothing to do with the decision to leave, Julia admits that she "hoped there would not be any more strange encounters during the last few weeks at the Speed." She also says, "I don't know what I would have done if I'd have experienced anything else weird in the Kentucky Room. I still don't believe in ghosts, but what I witnessed and felt inside that museum was very strange indeed."

Most people who have experienced these types of strange events at the Speed Museum, however, aren't quite as skeptical as Ms. Simpson, and whenever anything unusual or unexplained happens, employees generally agree that "it must have been Miss Hattie." Most seem to think of her as a benevolent, albeit jealous, spirit, yet there are those who also feel a malevolent force at work in the museum. In 1999 a psychic from California who had family in the Louisville area paid a visit to the Speed Museum and supposedly claimed that "a very evil force seemed to lurk on the stairs that led to the lower floor of the museum, and was somehow connected to some of the objects in the Native American collection." The man had planned the museum visit solely for pleasure and said he had no idea a ghostly encounter awaited him.

"I had separated from my friends and was alone on the stairs, walking down to the exhibits of Native American artifacts," he recounts of that early afternoon, "and I suddenly saw a man standing on the bottom step, but in a split second he was gone. And he had such an angry look on his face that it really frightened me." Although the figure vanished right away, the man from California said it appeared to be a Native American. "He had long black hair and dark, ruddy skin, like an Indian, but he wasn't in the stereotypical get-up they'd wear in the movies. It was more like a simple beige tunic that went down to his knees and a pair of trousers made from the same material." Other than a narrow headband, the startled psychic doesn't remember any details. He proceeded to the Native American room and felt a very strong, negative presence as he walked through the exhibit. "I tried to make mental contact with him, but I was unable to. I left and haven't been back since."

Connie Barber and Sue Holzbaum claim they saw a similar apparition on a visit to the Speed in 2002. The two women in their early thirties work at the University of Louisville and remember the day they went for lunch at the popular cafe in the museum. "We had just finished lunch and headed out the front entrance, through the main lobby," explains Connie, "when we realized we still had some time left. So we decided to go downstairs and look around. We had seen most of the

museum before, but had never been to the Indian stuff downsta__
two women took a quick look around the gallery, and after ten n__
they decided to leave. As they approached the stairs leading up t__
lobby, Sue saw what appeared to be a statue in the corner. Surprised th__
they had overlooked it, she paused to examine it, but then froze. "I realized it wasn't a statue!" she says. "It was a real person, an Indian man
with long black hair and brown skin! I was scared, so I grabbed Connie's
arm, and she just gasped when she saw it!"

The two women stood and watched while what they assumed to
be a real person vanished in front of them. Connie says, "I could have
sworn it was a real person. He looked totally natural, but just out of date.
And just as plain to see as the nose on your face!" The ladies left and say
they haven't returned to the Speed Museum since then. "We've actually
heard *tons* of stories about strange things going on at that museum,"
claims Barb, "so I'm not really all that shocked it happened. It sounds
crazy, I know, and if anyone told me the story I just told, I probably
wouldn't believe them. But that's what happened! We know what we
saw."

ABOUT THE SPEED MANSION

The Speed family counts as one of the most well-known and
prominent families in Louisville. James Breckinridge Speed was born in
Missouri in 1844 and died in 1912 at his summer home in Rockland,
Maine. His parents and grandfather hailed from Kentucky, and he himself came to Louisville at the age of eleven. He studied at Louisville Male
High School and went to work in a bank at the age of sixteen. Mr. Speed
enlisted with an Ohio regiment in the Volunteer Army of the United
States in 1861, later becoming Adjutant of the 27th Kentucky Regiment
during the Civil War.

Returning to Louisville after the war, J.B. Speed became super-
intendent of the Louisville Cement Company, and then its president. As

building of extensive cement works in Clark
...nization of a successful coal business, and the
...uisville Street Railway Company. He even-
...he Ohio Valley Telephone Company and
...one in his home at 505 West Ormsby

...ps that's why an old-fashioned telephone can still be heard
...ng in various parts of the building, even though all the present-day
phones seem to be thoroughly modern. Built in 1883 by Dexter

Reputedly the first house in the city to have a telephone, the sprawling Speed Mansion on Ormsby Avenue was built by local architect Dexter Bellknap in 1883. The unexplained sounds of an old-fashioned telephone can still be heard today.

Belknap, the sprawling mansion at 505 West Ormsby Avenue did enjoy the reputation as the first home in Louisville to have a telephone; however, the elegant home would be remembered for a more famous inhabitant, Harriet "Hattie" Speed. Miss Hattie, Speed's second wife and an accomplished concert pianist, lived in the house for many years after his death in 1912 and used the gracious front parlors as a music room where she gave lessons and held recitals for many years. Perhaps that's why the lovely strains of classical music from an invisible piano have been heard at all hours of the night in the refined rooms of one of Old Louisville's most revered homes.

Chapter 9

BROOK STREET

rook Street in the late 1800s counted as one of the most respectable upper-middle-class streets in Louisville. Lined with shade trees and large, unassuming, two-and three-story homes, many considered it the prime location for the town's merchants, bookkeepers and business managers, and even the odd lawyer or schoolmaster. As early developers sold off prime plots of land on Saint James Court and up and down Third and Fourth Avenues, the desirability of land in the area increased and extended the boundaries of the Derby City's most exclusive neighborhood. Although some of the Old Louisville elite may have felt that it had a definite *working-class* air about it, the residents of Brook Street certainly enjoyed a comfortable existence during Louisville's Gilded Age.

Victorians in the River City's upper class lived in a time when the influx of river trade and train travel inundated the city with an unprecedented degree of wealth and sophistication. This prosperity showed itself in an overabundance of impressive residential architecture that made Louisville a city famous for its comfortable and elegant homes. In 1909 *The Louisville Times* of December 31 reflected on the town's self-proclaimed title as the "City of Homes" in an end-of-the-year article describing national acclaim for her impressive residences. "Those who come to Louisville from afar return whence they came with an abiding admiration for the instinct that teaches men and women of Louisville to make the home the paramount interest of their lives. Proportionately to its size Louisville owns more handsome and livable homes than any other city in this country; and the instinct is still fully alive."

Within a matter of fifty years Louisville had transformed itself from wilderness outpost to a bustling river town, and by the time it reached its centennial in 1892, it had all the trappings of a modern-day American city. From newspapers and the arts, to luxury hotels and restaurants, science and industry, Louisville could compete with any town its size – or larger – in the nation. As industry prospered and generated wealth, the number of wealthy families dramatically increased, and as a result, so did the attention paid to social standing and perceptions of good taste and etiquette.

Just like its snootier neighbors on Third and Fourth Avenues, Brook Street strictly adhered to Victorian custom, and female residents observed "calling days," certain days of the week when ladies of the house on a certain street would stay home to receive visits from other ladies in the neighborhood. And even if they couldn't afford to keep a whole household staff like their neighbors in the mansions on Millionaires Row, people on Brook Street enjoyed their domestic help as well. If a butler, maid *and* housekeeper couldn't be afforded, a respectable family had to have at least a live-in maid to take care of the most menial chores.

Today's residents of Brook Street have long thought their street to be haunted by the ghost of one of these Victorian housemaids. A shadowy figure that appears just after nightfall, she has come to be known as *the Phantom of Brook Street*. Although actual descriptions of the ghost vary, they all have one thing in common: her clothing, said to be reminiscent of a maid's uniform in the 1800s. Observers have described seeing a young woman in a light gray, long-sleeved dress with a white lace apron and matching bonnet. Most can easily identify her as a maid or some type of servant girl from a foregone time. Witnesses also say she seems to float along the sidewalks at night, usually with her face turned away from the viewers, and they almost always hear a long, piercing scream before she vanishes into thin air.

Hattie Sullivan lived in a second-floor apartment near the corner of Brook and Oak Streets for many years, and she recalls a very similar scene on one summer evening as she gazed out of the window. Looking down at nothing in particular with her chin resting in her hands while her elbows rested on the windowsill, she couldn't sleep that night for some reason.

"I had gone to bed early, about 10:00, since I had worked late, and I was really tired," she explains. "But after I had dozed off, I woke with a sudden jolt because I heard someone scream. It was a woman, and it seemed to be a painful, blood-curdling scream. I lay there awake at first, not sure if I had dreamed it or really heard it. I was so riled up, that I couldn't sleep, so I got up out of bed and turned on the radio." With soft tunes floating from the AM channel, Hattie walked over to the window where she had a good view of the intersection below and decided to take a look. She saw nothing unusual, just the occasional car or bus driving by, and maybe a college student or two returning home after night classes, but she enjoyed her little corner and what excitement it offered every now and then. Besides, she didn't have a TV, so other than books and the radio, this provided her main form of entertainment when at home.

"I just propped my elbows up on the window ledge like I always did," she explains, "and I just started to watch. I wasn't hoping to see anything in particular, just people walking by, neighbors coming and going, stuff like that... It was a really warm night, I remember. It was right after the Derby, and it was one of the first really warm nights we had that summer. I had been there for about ten or fifteen minutes when all of a sudden I got this really strange feeling. I was looking down Brook Street, towards downtown, and I noticed some of the streetlights had gone out. All I could see was our intersection and then sort of like a dark cave under the tree branches where the rest of the street disappeared. It was like the street just sort of disappeared into blackness. As I was looking down, trying to see how many streetlights had gone out, a cool breeze suddenly swept up the street, rustling all the leaves in the trees. It was like a really hot summer day, when a storm sneaks up on you and the first indication you get is when the wind turns cold."

Hattie says she expected to see rain fall soon, so she lowered the window a bit and pulled her housecoat tight around her. "I pulled it

Parts of Brook Street look the same as they did in 1887 when a local girl was murdered here. Residents still believe her spirit still roams this street.

tight under my chin and leaned over against the side of the window, waiting for the rain to come, but nothing happened. Instead, all I saw was this eerie glow coming from under the trees on my side of Brook Street. As I watched, it seemed to get brighter, and all the while the hair was standing up on the back of my neck, and the wind was still blowing hard. Then, like out of nowhere, I saw this figure come out of the darkness."

As a first reaction she wanted to retreat back into the safety of her apartment, out of view of whatever walked the street, but she seemed glued to the spot, transfixed by what she saw. "Out of the corner of my eye I could see the fireplace mantel on the wall next to me, and I just wanted to run over there and start a fire for some reason," she reports. "I don't know why, but I just wanted to go and light a fire. For some reason, I felt *so cold.* And I got such a bad case of goose bumps!" Even if she had managed to muster herself from her perch at the window and make it over to the fireplace, Hattie wouldn't have been able to start a fire anyway, since the flues had been closed up years before that. Nonetheless, she had a large, ornately carved fireplace mantel of maple and oak in her small bedroom, and she liked it because it reminded her that she lived in a house where rich people used to live.

"This figure I saw looked like a maid that might have worked in one of these houses way back when," she reports. "I knew right away I was definitely looking at a maid girl or servant because of her uniform. The dress was sort of plain and gray, but she had on a white apron with lace trim and a frilly bonnet like they used to wear in the 1800s. I couldn't see her hair or anything, but I had the impression that she was white, maybe with darker hair and eyes. And she was short. She just seemed to float out of the dark under the trees, surrounded by a strange, hazy yellow glow. I just watched her come down the sidewalk for what seemed like an eternity, but it probably lasted more like thirty or forty seconds. Then all of a sudden, she raised her hands to her face, and I heard the same terrible shriek that woke me up before that, and she just disappeared. The wind stopped blowing, and the street lamps came back on, and it was like nothing ever happened. It was nice and warm outside, but I still had goose bumps all over me."

Many witnesses to the Brook Street phantom report the same chilly wind, eerie glow and sense of longing that accompanied Hattie's sighting. Some even claim that the haunt, forlornly sobbing for some unknown reason and with her face in her hands, has hovered along the sidewalks of Brook Street. Many have suggested that these sightings involve the ghost of a young maid in search of a house to clean. Joe Grayson, an active member of the Louisville Paranormal Society and native Louisvillian, claims his grandmother, a longtime resident of Brook Street, referred to this ghost as "the *Old* Maid"; however, most agree that they get the distinct impression of a *young* woman.

Charlie Hutchins thinks that the spirit of a young woman who used to work in one of the homes no longer standing on Brook Street haunts the area. A spry octogenarian who has lived his entire life in the Old Louisville neighborhood, Charlie can recall references to the Brook Street Phantom from his days as a student at the old Male High School in the 1920s. He even claims to have seen an apparition that fits the description of a young Victorian housemaid.

Although the local school board almost demolished the structure in the mid 1990s, preservationists and neighborhood activists teamed up to save the significant landmark and today it serves a community center. When Charlie Hutchins attended in the 1920s, Male High School had just barely completed its first decade of existence. "Back then," he explains, "that was the place to go. If you lived downtown, you usually went to Male. The location was terrific. During our lunch break or after school let out, we'd head over to Fourth Street and hang out. Back then, that's where everyone went." Up until the 1950s and 1960s, Fourth Street served as the city's premier entertainment artery, offering locals and visitors alike a wide variety of theaters, clubs, cafes, restaurants and shops.

"We'd spend the whole afternoon walking up and down Fourth Street," Charlie recollects, "just window shopping and watching the girls and swapping stories. Saturdays were the best there, though. I'd get up early, do my chores at home, and then meet my friends in front of the Seelbach Hotel, and then we'd just walk up and down the street. The Great Depression was just starting, but to see Fourth Street back then, you'd never think there were any problems in the country. Everyone seemed happy."

During one of these Saturday walks up and down Fourth Street, a friend told him the story about the ghost of Brook Street. "I don't know if I really believed in spirits and haunts and such, but it was getting close to Halloween and we were making plans to sneak into the cemetery at night, so talk turned to witches and spooks." A classmate, Eddie, told him that a servant had been murdered in one of the houses near the school, and that her ghost supposedly walked the halls late at night.

"Other kids talked about this ghost, but I don't know that I ever believed any of it at that point. As for the story of the girl getting killed in one of the houses, that was something I had heard before, too. My dad had told me about that, so I pretty much believed it." Charlie says he became a believer in ghosts not too much longer after he had heard the stories that his friend Eddie had told him. "It was the middle of November and some of us had stayed after school to help the teacher get ready for the upcoming Christmas play. A bunch of guys were in the auditorium putting up decorations and I had to get some stuff from a storage room down the hall."

His arms full of rolls of green and red streamers, an uneasy feeling suddenly overcame him as he walked alone down the corridor. "I looked up, and right in front of me I saw this...*figure* or something...It was all white and looked to be a servant girl with an apron and bonnet. I stopped dead in my tracks, and she just seemed to stare straight ahead, almost looking right through me. And then she just started to fade away, and soon there was nothing at all. I ran back to the others and made sure I was never alone in those halls again."

Others have had even closer, and more unsettling, encounters with the ghost on Brook Street. One of them, Rhonda Buckman, a native of Louisville now lives on the East Coast. As a U of L dental student, she rented an apartment on Brook Street for five years in the early 1980s when in her late twenties. Although she had grown up in that part of town, she had never heard anyone talk about the Phantom of Brook Street. "My family was very Baptist and very conservative, so ghosts were out of the question for us," she explains.

Nonetheless, she cannot explain a strange series of events that happened to her while she lived in her Brook Street apartment almost twenty years ago. "I decided to get this apartment because, number one, the rent was cheap, and, number two, it was only a couple blocks from school. Some people thought me foolish for living in this part of town, but it didn't bother me at all." A tall, athletic girl, Rhonda played volleyball and loved to cycle when she had the time. She usually tried to get in a good jog around the neighborhood before it got dark, and before she had to crack the books for her classes the next day. When she needed a break, she liked to walk the several blocks to nearby Fort George on Floyd Street and relax on the solitary park bench in the middle of the small memorial garden.

"One day I got home about 5:30 that afternoon, after a quick jog over to Fort George and that neighborhood. Since it was fall, it was just getting dark. I had been in the apartment for about two months, and I pretty much had established a routine. I'd get home from class around 3:00, take a nap for an hour or so, do stuff around the house, jog for half an hour, come home, shower, fix something to eat, and then start to study. I'd usually go to bed around 2:00 in the morning. It was my second year of school, and I was really enjoying myself. I usually had lots of free time on the weekends, and I had a great apartment."

Although Rhonda's family had lived in a large, modern condominium in the city center, she had grown especially fond of her first-floor apartment in a large, three-story mansion somewhere in the 1300 or 1400 block of Brook Street. Although it had been divided into three spacious apartments, the hundred-year-old building had belonged to a well-to-do family until the 1930s, when the last member had sold it and moved to Florida for the warmer climate. From the abundance of rich woodwork, gleaming hardwood floors with inlay and elaborate fireplace mantels, the family obviously had spared no expense when building the house. Even though the plain, brick façade would never have betrayed its secrets, many considered the interior to be a bit ostentatious, at the least. The house also had an impressive grand stairway, an abundance of stained glass and polished brass, and even the maid reputedly enjoyed more than average comfort in her two-room quarters on the third floor.

"In my kitchen, which was the original kitchen of the house, there's a back stairway that leads straight up to where the servant lived on the third floor. Even though it was blocked off at the top of the stairs and no one could enter the stairs except from my kitchen, I never liked being on those steps. I always got a very strange feeling on those stairs." She had never experienced anything more than an uncomfortable feeling when she opened the door to the back stairway, but other renters had claimed to hear strange noises and sobs coming from that part of the house. "I never considered myself superstitious or anything, but I had heard stories that the third floor was haunted. Since I was on the first floor, I tried not to think about it too much. But, when I did have to get on the stairs, it did creep me out sometimes."

On the night in question, Rhonda had just opened the door to the servant's access stairs when she had the distinct feeling of someone watching her. "I kind of used the steps for extra storage because there weren't a lot of closets in the apartment, and I needed some clean dishtowels I usually kept in a basket on one of the lowest steps. As I opened the door and reached down for a towel, I froze. I could feel someone's eyes on my back, and it gave me chicken skin." Not sure of what she should do, she slowly closed the door and straightened up. "I wanted to turn around and look, but I knew if I did, I'd see someone."

Before she could muster her next thought, she heard a series of taps on the small window over the kitchen sink, and she couldn't help but spin around. "I was surprised that there was no one behind me, since the feeling I had was so strong, but my heart was still beating a hundred miles a minute. Sometimes people stop by unexpectedly, so I walked over to the sink and looked out the window, and there was no one there at all." She stopped to think for a minute, and wondered if maybe a friend was playing a trick on her, but then remembered that the small window over the kitchen sink had to be at least ten feet off the ground. Like many of the homes in the neighborhood, the house sat on stone foundations that raised the ground floor four or five feet above street level.

"At first, I was really spooked, but then I just convinced myself that I had imagined someone rapping at that window. I went ahead and made dinner and ate, and then cleaned up a bit before going into the living room to study for a couple hours. I had pretty much forgotten the whole episode." That is, until she walked into the living room and turned on the lights. In front of the fireplace, on the floor in the middle of the room, someone had taken two fireplace pokers and laid them in the shape of a cross.

"It felt so strange when I saw that!" she recalls. "It was like someone punched me in the stomach and knocked the wind out of me. I just gasped for air and ran out of the room. After a couple minutes I was finally able to pull myself together, and it was then that I realized that I was terrified!" She ran to a friend's house a couple of blocks away and brought him back to her apartment, where everything looked fine, except for the pokers that still rested on the floor in the living room. "I thought that somebody had broken in, but we looked around and couldn't find anything. It was then that my friend told me the story about the ghost on Brook Street."

It seems that Rhonda's friend, Tom, had lived on Brook Street most of his life, and he had grown up hearing stories about the 'Phantom of Brook Street.' "When I brought him back to the apartment," explains Rhonda, "he tried to convince me that I was imagining things or that someone I know had been in the apartment, but when he saw how scared I was, he started to take me seriously. He didn't really want to tell me anything, but when I pressed him, he gave in and told me what he had heard."

According to neighborhood lore, the lost spirit of a young girl still walks up and down the street. Perhaps she worked as a maid in one of the Brook Street residences in the late 1800s and hasn't found her employer's house yet. Tom's grandmother had told him that a woman servant in the late 1880s had been alone in the house and startled two burglars at the fireplace. They attacked her and savagely beat her, and a couple days later she died. Ever since then, people on the street have reportedly heard terrible moans and shrieks late at night, and some even claimed to have seen the apparition of a young female in a maid's uniform. Neighbors had also given accounts of strange occurrences in people's homes, and these reports almost always involved ghostly activity around the fireplace.

"When I heard about the fireplace, my blood turned cold!" confides Rhonda. "I really started to wonder about the place where I was living." Sensing her uneasiness, her friend offered to spend the night and make sure that nothing bad happened, an offer she quickly accepted. He needed to run home and get a change of clothes, and Rhonda said she would be fine for the five or ten minutes he'd be gone, however, when Tom returned he found a pale and visibly shaken Rhonda waiting at the front door.

"Listen!" She pointed back towards the kitchen, her hand shaking violently. Loud footsteps could be heard running up and down the stairs at the back of the house. "It started right after you left," she explained anxiously. "There must be someone in the back stairway." Cautiously, they both made their way to the kitchen and stopped in front of the door that opened onto the servant's stairs. They listened closely as what sounded like a pair of bare feet ran quickly up and then down the stairs before starting all over again.

"We just looked at each other and stared. I was shaking all over, and I could tell that Tom was freaked out, too, but he was trying to hide it." After what seemed like an eternity to her, and after she had convinced her male friend that no one could have entered the back stairs other than through her kitchen, he reached out and quickly yanked open the door.

"The second he opened the door, the footsteps stopped – just like that! It sounded sort of like they reached the top of the stair, and then just vanished." Standing at the bottom of the steps, the two looked up and into the empty stairwell as a rush of icy air quickly enveloped them. Only a dim 40-watt bulb hanging over the second floor landing lit the gloomy interior, casting long shadows on the outdated wallpaper as it slowly swung back and forth. Rhonda still can't find the words to describe the uneasy sensation that overcame her at the sight of the light fixture gently swaying in the empty stairwell. "It was so creepy that I almost fainted," she recalls.

Even after her friend had ascended the full two flights of stairs to make certain that the doors to both the second and third floors could not be opened, Rhonda couldn't rid herself of the apprehension that plagued her. "We left the apartment right after all the noise on the stairs, and I didn't come back for two days. When I finally did come back, I brought two girlfriends along and they stayed over the first night." Although she had calmed down a bit, Rhonda still had doubts about being alone in the apartment at night.

"As long as I had people around, it didn't bother me as much. I guess it made me feel better knowing that I had witnesses to whatever strange stuff went on there." She hoped that the running noises on the steps turned out to be a one-night affair, even if her skeptical friends didn't receive the proof they needed to convince them that she hadn't imagined the whole event. However, they too would soon become reluctant witnesses to the ghostly activity playing out in Rhonda's kitchen, no matter how hard she tried to keep them away from the back stairs that night.

"The minute I walked back into the apartment," she recalls, "I got that same awful feeling again, and I was sort of expecting something to happen again. We ordered pizza, so we really didn't need to be in the kitchen." The more skeptical of her friends insisted on checking out the servant's stairs for herself, so she made a beeline to the kitchen as soon as they entered the apartment, ran up the steps and tried to open the two doors that went to the other floors. "I told her they were nailed shut, but she had to check for herself. She wouldn't rule out the possibility that someone could have come through from the other side until I convinced her that I had been in the other apartments and seen it with my own eyes." Rhonda remembers that a new wall covered the door to the back stairs on the second floor and that the landlord had built a large set of shelves to cover the entrance on the top story. "I had thought of that possibility as well, so before I went back into the apartment, I talked with both of my neighbors and asked if they had heard anything strange that night." Neither of the tenants had heard anything that evening.

"Everything seemed fine and we ate our pizza, played cards and watched a little TV. It was a Friday night, and we didn't have to worry about classes the next day, so we also had a couple bottles of wine. We were all feeling pretty good when we stumbled to bed around 2:00 that morning." Rhonda remembers showing her friends to the large guest room that adjoined the living room next to hers and then falling fast asleep as soon as her head hit the pillow in her own bed. "I was in a very deep sleep, and I usually am a very light sleeper. I guess it was the combination of the wine and the stress from the two days before. I was out like a light."

She doesn't remember what woke her, but Rhonda recalls suddenly sitting upright in bed, staring out the door towards the kitchen. She could hear both her friends yelling, the panic in their voices very evident. "I shot out of bed and bolted for the kitchen, not really sure what to expect. I was so groggy and out of it, I couldn't even remember where I was." As she ran past the open door to the guest bedroom, she saw one of the girls sitting upright in the bed, a look of bewilderment and fear painted on her face. The large patchwork quilt lay on the floor. Her other friend stood in front of the door to the back stairs and stared down at the doorknob as it slowly turned around and around.

"I saw that door and the handle going around and around, and then I remembered where I was. It all came back to me and then I could hear the same steps as someone or something ran up and down the steps." Her friend just stared, her eyes wide in amazement as the brass knob kept rotating in the same direction. The woman in the bedroom slowly emerged, the quilt tightly around her body. Hair matted over to one side, it looked like she had just awoken from a very long sleep. "I asked what had happened, and she just shook her head and shrugged her shoulders. I could tell she was still asleep."

Rhonda later learned that the two had been fast asleep when someone yanked the large comforter off the bed they shared. They then heard the footsteps coming from the kitchen, and something that sounded like laughter. A woman's laughter…"I didn't hear anyone laughing," confides Rhonda, "but I did hear those footsteps again, that's for certain. The same creepy footsteps…" Her friend at the door still had her eyes transfixed on the spinning doorknob when she slowly reached out and took it in her hand. Taking a deep breath, she paused and then pulled the door open without effort. Rhonda says, "I told her not to open it, but she went ahead and did it anyway. I was afraid we might actually see something this time." They could see only the dark interior of the stairwell and the wicker basket Rhonda normally kept the towels in, as it *tumbled* slowly down the steps and landed upright on the tiled kitchen floor.

"It was like someone at the top of the stairs threw the basket down at us. We just kept staring at it on the floor, not knowing what to do." Trying to mask her fear, her friend grabbed a flashlight from one of the cupboards and then ran up the stairs. "She was convinced that somebody had run up the stairs, even when she reached the top and saw that both doors couldn't be opened. I could tell she was upset, but she just didn't want to admit that something strange had just transpired. She's the kind that thinks there has to be a logical explanation for everything." However, they could come up with no plausible explanation for the happenings in the kitchen of the old house on Brook Street. Nor could they rationalize the sight that awaited them in the living room when they returned to the comforting glare of the TV. Once again, the fireplace pokers lay in the shape of a cross in the middle of the floor…"Both my friends turned white when they saw the pokers crossed on the rug," recalls Rhonda. "We turned on the television and stayed up all night. They left the next morning and didn't want to come back."

For the next two weeks Rhonda stayed in the apartment off and on, always making sure that she had at least one other person with her at all times. "I was still scared," she readily admits. "It was bad enough when people were with me, and I didn't want to risk it all alone. Besides, my friends wouldn't have let me go back alone anyway. They were pretty concerned, especially when we started to hear the screams." The next Monday night, Rhonda, not able to sleep in spite of her exhausted physical and mental states, lay in bed. Tom and another friend slept soundly in the adjacent guestroom. "I was just starting to get drowsy when we heard this horrible scream all of a sudden. It sounded like it came from the kitchen, a woman's horrible, painful scream." By the time she ran to the kitchen, the two men had already turned on the lights and waited in front of the closed door to the back stairs. They all heard the same set of feet race quickly up and down the wooden steps, however, this time the footsteps sounded much louder and angrier, almost deliberately so.

"It sounded like *she* – or whatever it was – was really angry. The steps just kept getting louder and louder, like she was pounding her feet on purpose to let us know she wasn't happy. It eventually got so loud and violent that the girl on the floor above me heard it and came down to see what all the commotion was." Rhonda quickly explained the situation and escorted the other woman to the back of the house and showed her the back stairwell. Angry feet still stomped up the steps behind the closed door, and the four individuals gathered there could discern the barely audible moans of someone at the top of the stair, faintly sobbing. "Of course, we opened the door again, and like before, there was no one there at all. Even though we had replaced the light bulb from the time before, it was burnt out again, and the two guys had to use a flashlight to see their way to the third story." Unlike the previous disturbances, however, no one hurled the basket at them or set the light to swinging on its chain. The two men did report a spot of icy air at the top landing and a strange mist-like fog that materialized and hung over the spot for a minute or two before vanishing. They noted a strange scent lingering in the air as well, a sickly sweet floral aroma reminiscent of the orchids and lilies sent for funerals. "I just took them at their word," clarifies Rhonda. "There was no way at all I was going up those steps!"

Suddenly, they all jumped and turned around, startled by several loud knocks on the window over the kitchen sink behind them. Much louder and more violent than the soft taps Rhonda had heard that first night, these raps threatened to shatter the glass pane. Rhonda's friend Tom bolted to the sink, followed by the other man. A bright outdoor floodlight illuminated the small back yard, and at the window, the two men could see nothing at all out of the ordinary. Dry leaves over the patch of ground beneath the window lay undisturbed, and an old brick carriage house with weathered gingerbread trim offered no way of escape since a rusty old padlock secured the solitary door that opened onto the back yard. "The four of us ended up in the back garden, and it was easy to see that if someone had been there, they would have had a very hard time leaving. The back door into my apartment and the door to the old carriage house are the only two ways to get out. The other two sides are bounded by very high – and dense – holly hedges with chain link running through them."

Clustered around the moss-covered stone fountain, the small group stood in the middle of the back garden while the men debated the practicality of a return to the apartment. As she pulled the blanket closer around her, Rhonda listened only half-heartedly, her eyes drawn to the small window over the sink that looked into her kitchen. Her skin prickled with nervousness and the first signs of fall in the chilly air, she let her eyes wander up and across the towering back façade of the building and then let her gaze rest on one of the second floor windows. Her eyes slowly focused and she quickly inhaled a long gasp of air. She could discern a vague form standing at the window and it seemed to be looking down at them.

"It looked like the shape of a young girl or a child with a frilly bonnet, but I couldn't really make anything else out," she recalls. "It was definitely a person, that's for sure, but it looked very one-dimensional, as if I was looking at a sheet of fog or mist. It kind of hovered there and flickered or shimmered. It's very hard to describe…"

Her startled gasp drew the attention of the others, and they all found themselves staring up at the strange figure in the window. The diaphanous form of a woman in light gray seemed to float in the darkness of the windowpane, keeping close watch over the four individuals below. She appeared to lift her hands and cover her face, and then vanished.

"We just figured that we had experienced yet another strange phenomenon – one of many that week – and I guess we didn't know what to do. We were just going to wait and see, I suppose, but then, all of a sudden my friend Tom turned completely white. He was staring up at the window and he was white as a sheet." According to Rhonda, Tom had figured out what it was about that window that had been bothering him. "At first he, just like the rest of us, assumed the window belonged to the apartment on the second floor. But the more he stared at it and went over things in his head, the more he realized that it couldn't be a window to the second-floor apartment." Tom had figured out that the window had to be in the same spot as the second-floor landing in the back stairway, the *servant's stairs.* He also recalled that he had seen no windows whatsoever along the back steps leading up from Rhonda's kitchen.

The next five or ten minutes seemed to float by, as Rhonda recalls, and every minute has been indelibly etched in her memory. "It almost felt like I was in a movie…but watching everything from the outside." When they all realized that the window had to lead somewhere, the small group ran back to the kitchen and then up the stairs to the small landing on the second story. The sound of feet running up and down the steps had ceased, and the lone bare bulb that hung overhead had not burned out this time. "We all stood there, crammed together on the landing, and tried to figure out where that window could have been," she explains, "but it was obvious that there were no windows in the stairwell." Finally, they started to run their hands over the tattered wallpaper in the hopes of feeling something hidden underneath. In older dwellings such as this one, property owners often boarded up or otherwise obscured unnecessary or cumbersome interior windows, so they decided to at least try and find something. Rhonda found a small indentation in the wall about four feet off the ground and started to work her fingers through the moldy paper until her index finger hooked a small latch lying flat in a vertical recess. "I pulled on it, and a section of wallpaper started to tear away as a small door came open a bit. We ripped off all the paper that was covering it, and then yanked on the door some more, but it was really hard to open. It must have been years since it was last opened, so it had lost its square and the bottom really scraped against the floor."

Three of them managed to heave and pull till the door had cracked wide enough for someone to slide through the opening. Inside, by the light of a flashlight, they discovered a small room probably used as a cleaning closet or utility room at one time when the original family occupied the house. Although squirrels and pigeons had definitely felt at home there, it seemed that people hadn't used the space for seventy or eighty years. Old mops and brooms still rested against the wall, and soap and cleanser in their original boxes sat on bare wooden shelves. Local newspapers spanning two decades lay in a heap on the floor, the most recent of which gave details about the "Great Loss of Life" and "Immeasurable Human Suffering" after the sinking of the Titanic in

1912. Several tattered items of clothing, rendered almost unrecognizable after years of neglect and decay, hung on a wooden peg next to the small window that looked out over the back garden. One appeared to be a shapeless gray smock or tunic, the other was a small white apron, its lace trim still crisp and neat.

After that night, Rhonda says the strange activity in her old apartment on Brook Street stopped completely. She and her friends heard no more footsteps up and down the back stairs, and they heard no raps at the window. The fireplace pokers stayed put in their stand to the left of the mantel in the living room, and Rhonda never again experienced that uneasy feeling she sometimes had in the kitchen near the back stairs. "After we discovered that secret little closet off the landing, all the weird stuff stopped. It was like she wanted us to find that room for some reason. Was she a maid in search of her next assignment? Did a servant really die a tragic death on this street long ago? I don't know…But I do hope she or whatever it was we saw that night in the window is at peace now."

Although Rhonda claims that research about that specific house yielded no evidence of foul play or tragedy in its past, I did dig up accounts from city newspapers in 1887 that give some credibility to the notion that the spirit of a young servant girl might haunt Brook Street. On April 21st, 1887, a twenty-three-year-old housemaid living in the home of the Mr. A. Y. Johnson family at 1522 South Brook startled two burglars as she came down the stairs into the dining room. Described as "a stout, healthy young woman of impeccable reputation," Jennie Bowman had been left in charge of the house that morning while Mrs. Johnson and her children paid nearby relatives a visit. Thinking the residence empty, Albert Turner and William Patterson, two local thugs, had entered and started searching for valuables when Jennie Bowman startled them. Although she did put up a brave fight, the two criminals attacked her and beat her terribly.

A short time later, the Johnson's son returned home to retrieve something his mother had forgotten. Seeing the door was locked, he crawled through a window and saw that the place was a "ghastly shambles." He quickly scrambled out and returned with his mother and neighbors, who found "pools of blood all over the floor, glass broken, furniture much displaced and rugs scattered about." Upstairs they found

Jennie Bowman lying on a bed, where her attackers had left her, just barely clinging to life.

The two doctors attending her, W.O. Roberts and J.S. Haskins, reported shock at the extent and savagery of the young girl's injuries. She had "three skull fractures, with her face and features completely disfigured, and finger prints on her neck." Most disturbing of all were reports that the two criminals had beat her around the head and shoulder with fireplace pokers, and that one of them struck her such a powerful blow to the cranium that it dislodged an eyeball from its socket. Even though she did succumb to her injuries a couple of weeks later, she reportedly had several lucid moments when she was able to give a remarkably accurate description of her attackers. In an ironic turn of fate, she was able to mar the face and seal the doom of one of her assailants, just as he had done to her. In her last act of bravery before losing consciousness, she had grabbed a broken wine goblet and raked it across the face of William Patterson, permanently branding him a killer.

With this information to go on, police soon apprehended the man and his accomplice, and took them to the old Jefferson Street jail to await trial. Louisvillians became so incensed as word and details of the horrible crime spread that a vicious mob soon formed and tried to storm the gates of the old city jail. Newspapers carried daily updates on the girl's progress and sensational accounts of the search for the killers, and Governor Proctor Knott and city authorities became so alarmed at the situation that they had the men moved to Frankfort to await trial. Within a year both had been tried, convicted and hanged, and Louisville eventually returned to normal after one its most brutal crimes and worse cases of civil unrest.

Today little remains concerning the tragic story of Jennie Bowman, other than several weeks' worth of newspaper articles and various accounts of the Brook Street phantom. Although the residence at the time had the address of 1522 South Brook Street, it doesn't pay to go looking to 1522 South Brook Street today for answers. In an effort to deal with the city's massive expansion and keep up with the influx of new homes in its first suburb, Old Louisville, the local government passed an ordinance in 1906 that changed the street-numbering system. The original house where the crime occurred occupied a spot not too far from Broadway and has long since been demolished. A stretch of I-65 covers that entire block, which – curiously enough – sits directly across from the old Male High School.

ABOUT OLD MALE HIGH SCHOOL

Across the street from the former Johnson residence, the site of Victorian Louisville's most heinous crime, sits Old Male High School, a majestic 1914 structure that fortunately survived several recent short-sighted attempts to bulldoze it. Today it stands proudly and – even though it technically lies outside the borders of Old Louisville – it has become an anchor for the Old Louisville community. Visitors can stop by and take in various concerts hosted there, get a bite to eat at a neighborhood restaurant or get tickets for the new dinner theater. Although the building is not used as a school anymore, people in the neighborhood are quite happy that the old structure is alive and well.

However, it seems that when the lights go down in this local landmark, the building takes on a life of its own. A laborer who stayed late one night to complete some renovation work claims he turned off every light in the enormous building before he locked up and ran to his car in the parking lot. But he says his heart almost jumped up in his throat when he pulled out onto the street in front of the old school and saw every single window ablaze with light. He ran back inside and spent ten minutes turning out the lights. When he entered the large auditorium – the last part of the building he needed to turn off – he claims he saw a strange man in white staring down at him from the interior balcony. He faded away into nothingness after a few seconds. When the disturbed worker left the second time, he made sure he drove out a back way so he wouldn't have to pass in front of the school

Several people claim they have heard mysterious groans late at night when they were the only people in the building, and they agree that it didn't sound like pipes or anything else mechanical that can sometimes be blamed. Some have attributed the strange noises to the ghost of Jennie Bowman, the young servant girl who was brutally attacked across the street in the late 1880s, but the spirit of a former student apparent-

Old Male High School sits across the street from the former A.Y. Johnson residence, the site of Victorian Louisville's most infamous crime. The spirit of a former pupil, among others, is said to haunt its hallowed halls.

ly survives as well. An old school legend claims that a former student beaten to death by his father in the 1920s still walks the hallowed halls of the imposing structure.

Marie Sandoval worked for a child care center housed in the old schoolhouse and she claims to have received a disturbing visit from the unfortunate boy one night. "We were usually closed and gone by 6:30 p.m. But one night I went home and realized I had left my purse behind. My husband and I had gone out for dinner and we stopped on the way home so I could get it." Marie recalls the exact time she entered the building to retrieve her bag that evening. "It was exactly ten after ten, and it was really dark and spooky outside. I ran to my desk and got my purse from the drawer, and as I was reaching for my keys I looked up and saw this little boy looking at me."

At first Sandoval was overcome with fear that a child had been left behind at the daycare center, but when she got a closer look at the boy, she realized that wasn't the case. "I saw that his face was all bruised, and there was blood all over his head and on his hands. He was ghastly pale and almost blue. I just shrieked and ran out of the building to my husband in the car. He didn't believe me and said I had drunk too much at dinner." But at work the following Monday, Marie says she shared her story with a coworker who had had a similar experience and described the same apparition.

Several other individuals in the Old Male High School claim that they have witnessed paranormal activity in certain parts of the building, including levitating objects, unexplained cold spots, and loud moans and sobs. Could they be the sobs of a young boy beaten to death by his father many years ago? Could they be the sad moans of a poor servant girl who died in agony in the late 1880s? Many neighborhood residents feel that these are secrets only the Old Male High School can tell.

ABOUT FORT GEORGE

Despite its grand Victorian traditions, the Old Louisville Neighborhood does have a small bit of colonial history to add to the mix. On a spacious plot of land on the 1200 Block of Floyd Street,

almost hi...
ment p...
marl...
fri...

Sr...

Could they be ...
Revolutionary war hero
George Gray and his wife,
Mildred?

dden behind a low wrought-iron fence, a small granite monu-
placed there in 1947 by the Daughters of the American Revolution
s the spot where Fort George once stood. Named for George Gray,
end of George Washington and Revolutionary War hero, the estate and
grounds were home to Gray and his wife, Mildred, when they returned
to Kentucky in the early 1800s. Now bounded by smaller shotgun structures, the tiny park has a narrow path leading visitors to two unassuming
headstones that mark the final resting spot of the Grays. On foggy mornings, neighbors and passersby have reported a colonial gentleman with
powdered wig and waistcoat emerging from the mist and then vanishing.
When winter has robbed the elms and chestnut trees of their leaves, and
only bare branches block out a gray, dreary sky, locals claim they have
heard the gallop of horses' hooves across the frozen ground near their
houses. On other occasions, neighbors have heard a lovely lady's voice
with an English accent singing old American folk songs. Have colonial
specters from the past returned to explore the present in America's largest
Victorian neighborhood?

Chapter

539
WEST SAINT CATHERINE

One of the major thoroughfares in Old Louisville, Saint Catherine Street unfortunately lost much of its original residential charm in the years following World War II when an interstate highway sliced its way south from the downtown and destroyed scores of beautiful old homes. The stretch of street running west from Third to Sixth Streets has remained largely unchanged and affords visitors several picture-perfect vistas of the best Old Louisville has to offer. From west to east, two rows of tidy brick townhouses frame the lacy façade of the Methodist Church, a Victorian masterpiece built of limestone and brick in 1884. Looking back to the west one can see the spires of Saint Louis Bertrand Catholic Church, another Old Louisville landmark of stone and brick erected in 1869.

The street had gained such a favorable reputation as a comfortable residential enclave that by the late 1880s many of the master craftsmen and designers employed to work on the more prestigious mansions on Third, Fourth and Ormsby Avenues decided to construct their own homes there. Several famous architects of the time even made their homes on West Saint Catherine. Kenneth McDonald lived at 514, for example, and L. Pike Campbell lived at 517. Another one, Cornelius A.

built a large house for his family in 1885, one supposedly mod-
after a large manor house he remembered from his childhood in
land. A solid three-story structure built of red brick with attractive
stone trim and a unique wooden exterior pocket door, it still stands at
539 West Saint Catherine Street today. Although the years have
obscured much of the history about the house at 539 West Saint
Catherine Street, Jon Huffman and Barb Cullen believe these basic facts
about their home and neighborhood to be true.

An energetic couple in their 40s, Barb and Jon purchased the
3,800-square-foot house in 2000 and set out to make it their home. Like
many transplants to Old Louisville, the two had started with a smaller
house and – after succumbing to the area's charm – decided to buy one
of the grander homes in need of some attention. Not only would the
house at 539 West Saint Catherine serve as a comfortable home where
they could entertain their many friends and family members, it would
also be a place they could ply their trades. Barb, a choreographer and
dancer, could give lessons from a room she used as a studio, and Jon, an
actor and screenwriter, could do his work from the home office on an
upper floor. After some repairs and remodeling, they would move in and
set up house. Little did they know that they would not be the only residents in the lovely brick house at 539 Saint Catherine Street.

Self-proclaimed skeptics of anything dealing with the paranormal, Jon and Barb never expected that they would one day come to
believe their own house was haunted. They had heard plenty of local
ghost stories and legends, but they always seemed, nonetheless, a bit far-
fetched to their sensibilities. The idea of an otherworldly entity in their
own house had never even entered their minds when they finally moved
in. When items in their new house started disappearing and reappearing
in strange locations, and when they heard loud, unexplained crashes,
they chalked it up to overactive imaginations and nothing else. In addition, workers still hadn't finished the final touches on the interior, so it
seemed that someone could always be blamed for the frequent loud
crashes and strange noises.

One evening the two found themselves at home when the loud
crash of shattering glass echoed somewhere in the house. Jon ran into the
kitchen, and, seeing that Barb wore the same shocked look on her face,
asked her if she had heard something. Nervously, they both searched the

house, realizing that for the first time since they had moved in, they were truly alone. Finding nothing, they both agreed it had sounded like a large light fixture or chandelier falling from the ceiling and crashing to the floor. From that point forward, the two started to take more notice of the sounds in the house around them; however, the reoccurring, unexplainable rattling of glasses clinking together or the faintly audible moans and shouts they repeatedly heard hardly made them think they had disembodied spirits in their home. That didn't happen till they experienced more than just sounds.

Jon and Barb can each recall one distinct incident that stopped them both cold in their tracks at the realization that some paranormal activity might be at play at 539 West Saint Catherine. For Jon, the incident was a rather simple, albeit unnerving, one. He had just walked in from a morning of errands and placed a bag of fresh bagels from a corner bakery on a counter in the kitchen. He hung up his jacket, put away his keys and ran up to his office to get in a couple hours work before lunch. When one o'clock rolled around, he went back down to the kitchen for a quick bite. Opening the door to the refrigerator, he sensed something wasn't quite right. Looking back over his shoulder, he realized someone had removed the bag of bagels from the counter. Scratching his head, he searched the kitchen from top to bottom but found nothing. He even returned to the car in the driveway, hoping that he had merely forgotten and left them inside, but still no bagels.

"For a half hour I searched up and down, and I just couldn't find that bag of bagels," he recalls. "I thought I had imagined the whole thing." Jon fixed himself a fast lunch, ate while he watched the news on TV, and then ran back upstairs to finish his work. He busied himself in his office for a couple of hours and then decided to take a quick bathroom break and call it a day. Walking down the hall to the bathroom, he never expected the sight that awaited him in the bathroom. Jon pushed open the door, and there, in the middle of the white, tiled floor, he spied the six bagels that had gone missing. Now out of the white paper bakery bag he had carried them in, they had been stacked neatly one atop the other to form a little column of bread that stood perfectly straight before him.

"It was so creepy," he remembers, "all I could do was stand there and stare. It was obvious that someone had done this, and I started to

An Old Louisville medium claims the spirit of young girl who died of TB in the 1920s still inhabits the house at 539 West Saint Catherine.

think for the first time that something supernatural might be going on in our house."

Barb says those same thoughts ran through her head one day when she walked into her dance studio after a quick trip to the kitchen.

Alone in the house, she had just given a dance lesson and wanted to tidy up a bit before her next pupil arrived. "I remember it very well," she explains, "because I had just picked up a small picture book and jump rope I keep in the studio for some of the younger kids and put it back in its spot under the TV. I was sort of irritated because I was always finding them in the middle of the floor and putting them back." When she went back into the studio, she froze, because the jump rope and book she had just placed under the TV once again lay in the middle of the floor. "That's when it hit me that something or someone was playing with me."

Whatever had caught Jon and Barb's attention this way seemed to them to be of a very mischievous nature, almost childlike or juvenile, and for this reason they claim they never really felt afraid or threatened ... at first. "For the most part, it was little things like the book and jump rope moving around and stuff, and things disappearing. And it seemed that it happened most on the bottom floor, like in the kitchen and the studio," says Barb, adding that she even started to get a feel for it and knew when to expect its antics. "I finally realized that most of the stuff happened when I was in the kitchen, cleaning, or right afterwards. It was strange. I noticed at other times weird things would happen after children had come to the house."

Another incident that caught Jon off guard and really gave him the "creeps" happened one day while he sat at his writing table on a cool fall evening in October. He had just come in from an afternoon with Barb strolling around the neighborhood and admiring the brilliant fall foliage and needed to take care of some matters at his desk. Barb had run to the grocery to get a few items for dinner, and he hoped that they'd have the time to catch a movie afterwards. Somewhat thirsty after his long walk, Jon decided to run to the kitchen for a cold drink. A minute or two later, he returned and stopped dead in his tracks as he approached the writing table. There, in the middle of the table, stood the pencil Jon had just put down. However, as he explains, "it was *literally* standing there, upright and perfectly straight, balancing on the eraser end." Although he admits that this stunt raised the hair on the back of his neck, he had to chuckle in spite of himself because he got the definite impression that someone had played a joke on him.

When the couple found themselves on the second floor, howev-

164

Ghosts of Old Louisville

er, they got a completely different vibe, and according to Jon, it wasn't a good one. "There was a large linen closet across from the bedroom on the second floor, and we never really felt comfortable around it," he explains. A plant lover with a huge green thumb, Jon first sensed this when he started to notice that perfectly healthy houseplants he had placed near the window in the linen closet had the unfortunate tendency of dying there, sometimes overnight. All over the house, plants thrived and flourished, but in this one room, he couldn't manage to keep anything alive, no matter how hard he tried. "It was puzzling, that's for sure. That closet really started to worry me when I noticed the animals acting strange around it," adds Barb.

Barb and Jon have three pets – two cats and one dog – and they noticed right after moving in that their companions displayed a clear aversion to the linen closet. "You couldn't make them go inside," explains Barb, "no matter how hard you tried. They hated it. They even hated walking past it in the hallway." Rocky, their lovable dog, had even been seen to pivot his entire body as he passed the doorway so as to keep the interior of the closet in sight at all times, a low growl in his throat as he did so. The couple's two cats – the best of friends before the move to 539 West Saint Catherine – seemed to act strange around it as well, and according to Barb, she often heard them hissing and screeching at each other, something that hadn't happened before. All three of them seemed to get spooked now and then in the bottom part of the residence as well, but it didn't compare to the reactions they showed when around the second-floor linen closet.

As the accounts of the strange occurrences spread among Barb's and Jon's friends and family, someone suggested that the couple call in a psychic or medium to get a reading of the house. Still skeptical of all things paranormal, they hesitated at first, but acquiesced after some friends went ahead and scheduled a psychic visit without telling them. "She had a good reputation," says Barb, "and by the time they told us she was coming, it was too late anyway. She was coming the next night." It was a cold January night, and the skeptical homeowners at 539 West Saint Catherine could not have anticipated the shock they would soon receive.

The following evening at 8:00 sharp the doorbell rang. Barb answered the door and showed the visitor in, impressed both by her neat appearance and self-assurance. A lively woman in her 40s named Cheryl, she had come to do a "cold reading" where no prior information whatsoever about the house or the strange events had been given. They all said their hellos, and Cheryl then got down to work. Standing in the inviting foyer, she took a long look around her and seemed to admire the surroundings – a huge oak staircase, lovely sliding pocket doors and delicate inlay in the gleaming hardwood floors. After several moments of silence, the psychic turned her attention back to Barb and Jon and asked a question. "What was going on here last week that brought so many children together?"

Dumbfounded at first, the couple didn't know how to respond since they hadn't anticipated that type of question. When Cheryl rephrased the question, they realized she had to be asking about a party they had thrown on the first of January. Over the years Barb and Jon had always thrown a large New Year's Day party at their house for family and friends, and it had become an annual tradition that carried over to the new house on West Saint Catherine As usual, a lot of children had been present at the latest gathering. When Barb shared this information with the psychic, she gave a simple reply: "Oh...that's why the little girl who still lives here was so happy."

The couple exchanged nervous glances and intently watched the psychic, who slowly closed her eyes, took a long, deep breath, and raised a hand to her neck. As if sensing the unspoken question that hung on their lips, *"What little girl...?"* she went on and told them she had made contact with a young girl who had lived in the house many years ago. Her parents had named her Rose, and she was eleven years old. She had red hair and blue eyes, and she loved to play...especially with other children her age. Cheryl informed them that when the house was full of kids the week before, the little girl was so happy to have someone to play with.

As they listened, Jon and Barb both realized that a fine layer of goose flesh had covered their bodies. "Jon!" Barb exclaimed in a hushed voice. "The pictures! The pictures from the party!" Barb wanted to run to a nearby drawer and pull out the pictures from the last few parties they had thrown in the house, but the psychic calmly raised a hand with the palm facing out to let them know she needed silence and stillness. Barb stopped and stayed where she was, deciding she could get the photos after the lady had finished her reading, even though the suspense was unbearable. Jon's eyes widened as he realized what pictures she wanted to see. Although he had convinced himself that a paranormal investigation of any sort would be a waste of time, he realized he needed to take this woman seriously.

Jon and Barb followed as Cheryl circled the foyer in a trance-like state and made her way to the parlor and then the dining room, making brief utterances now and then as she "received" information. In the dining room, she slowed her pace and cocked her head while the faintest hint of a smile spread across her face. "Yes, she likes to play, all right ..." remarked the psychic. Barb looked at Jon, and then they both looked under the television set in the corner of the room. The jump rope and picture book were still in place. Cheryl made for the door, but paused for a moment while she furrowed her eyebrows and appeared to listen while an unheard voice plied her with information. "She loves your pets and doesn't mean to scare them, she just wants to play with them," she commented. "Rose says she'll try not to scare them next time." Cheryl swept past Jon and Barb, unaware of the stunned looks on their faces, and entered the hallway leading into the kitchen.

She crossed the threshold into the kitchen and once again slowly canvassed the room in a relaxed, almost dreamlike state while getting a feel for the space and picking up whatever signals or vibes came her way. She stopped at the narrow stairs leading to the next floor and took a step, but then hesitated and stopped. She seemed to shake her head and back away, heading instead to the counter on the other side of the room. Stopping in front of the sink, the hand around her neck seemed to tighten, and her breath appeared to become shallow and labored. "Oh...It was *so hard* for her to breathe..." Cheryl now wore a pained look on her face, and sadness could be heard in her voice. "She was a very sick little girl. There was something wrong with her lungs. Probably tuberculosis ..." She paused a moment, and seemed to concentrate before looking in Barb's direction. "She doesn't like it when you clean the sink. She says the cleaner you use hurts her lungs." Dumbfounded, Barb watched as the psychic opened her eyes and appeared to come out of her trance-like condition. "That's all I get from her. Rose is gone for now," she said, and then walked back down the hall to the foyer at the front of the house.

Barb and Jon followed, silently pondering the revelations they had just heard. Like so many residents in the area, they hailed originally from somewhere other than Louisville – Barb, from Cincinnati, and Jon, from North Carolina – and considered Louisville their *new* hometown. They had both spent half their lives in the Derby City, and this being the case, they had both heard many stories about the infamous TB sanatorium at nearby Waverly Hills, supposedly one of the, if not *the*, most haunted locations in the United States. Thousands of men, women and children died there in the first years alone after it was built in 1926. Jon wondered to himself if Rose had been one of those unfortunate victims and started to form a mental image of her in his mind. He could see a small child in an old-fashioned, summery dress, frail perhaps, but cheerful, her long red hair done up in ribbons.

Cheryl had reached the foyer and started to ascend the stairs to the second floor. When she reached the landing, she paused and looked back down over the entry hall, apparently resuming her trance. She cocked her head and listened to something unseen while Barb and Jon looked on. They had assumed the woman had completed her psychic investigation and hadn't expected her to continue her way through the house. Cheryl mounted the remaining flight of stairs to the floor above and informed the two of them that she had made contact with another spirit, that of an elderly lady who had lived in the house. Once again Barb and Jon exchanged glances. They hadn't bargained on *two* ghosts in their house!

Cheryl mentioned that the old woman moved around a lot inside the house, and that she went in and out of the house a lot as well. "She's telling me something was not right with her medication," the psychic informed them. It seems that the unhappy woman suspected her grandson of changing pills around in her prescription bottles, or even poisoning her, because he wanted the old woman out of the picture. Her suspicions rose when she started to notice that various heirlooms and valuable antiques began disappearing. Once again, Jon and Barb exchanged surprised looks. They had both heard neighborhood stories about an old woman dying under mysterious circumstances, perhaps poisoned by her own grandson.

Cheryl continued her self-guided tour through the house, the two homeowners following in silence as she slowly and methodically made her way through one room after another. Every now and then she would stop and pause, her head turning as if she had heard something far off in the distance, her lips parting as if she wanted to speak, but then she would close her mouth and resume her wandering. A half hour later, they all stood together at the back of the hall on the second floor, still not a word having been spoken. Almost hesitant, Cheryl looked towards the only part of the house she hadn't visited – the linen closet – and then squinted her eyes before slowly making her way to the half-opened door. Although nothing had been said, Barb and Jon sensed that the psychic had deliberately avoided the small room until now. Trailing behind, they caught up with her as she stopped and pushed the door all the way open. She hesitated a minute and then cautiously stepped into the closet.

A small window on the back wall allowed a bit of light to shine in from the street, but other than that, there was no illumination. To the left, a shiny coat of beige paint shimmered softly on a smooth plaster wall. To the right, a tall bank of oak cupboards and drawers spanned the twelve feet of wall that rose from floor to ceiling. Enveloped in silence, Cheryl waited in the tiny space, unmoving and still. With Jon and Barb watching from the hallway, she lowered her head a bit and then twisted it to one side as if a loud noise had pierced her ears. She raised her head, turned and quickly exited the room with a shudder. Half way down the corridor, she stopped and turned to face the couple she had left standing outside the door.

"There are five *entities* in that room," she informed them, "and I'm getting some *very* negative vibes from them." She pivoted and then bolted down the stairs to the foyer. Glancing over her shoulder she added, "They're extremely hostile. I've asked them to leave, but they won't." Barb and Jon both cast a quick glimpse in the direction of the linen closet, and then bolted down the stairs after her. Down below they found the psychic, visibly shaken but in the process of regaining her composure.

Jon sat on the bottom stair and considered the situation. By the latest count he and his partner had seven disembodied spirits to contend with, and truth be told, he wasn't quite sure what one did in a situation like this, especially since he had gone from skeptic to believer in a matter of minutes. He looked at Barb, who in turn looked at Cheryl. "So, what should we do?" she inquired. The psychic studied the two of them for a moment and gave them a measured response.

"The energy in that room is *very* negative," she explained with a serious look. "It's very dark and very overpowering. I've never encountered such an overwhelming sense of animosity and anger before. You walk in and it's black and stifling, and it's like they're brooding about something. I've never had to deal with that before." As she spoke, her tone remained steady and severe, and she never took her eyes off of them. "They're *very* stubborn, as well," she added with a slight sigh. She relaxed a bit and then waited for them to speak.

The two, in turn, just stared at each other, but Jon did manage a feeble shrug of the shoulders in response. Still overwhelmed by the revelation of these new cohabitants, he found himself at a loss for words. Barb, torn between feelings of anxiety and dread at the sinister nature of the forces in her linen closet and a sense of relief because they had at least put a face – so to speak – on the powers responsible for the disturbances in their house, asked the psychic if they needed to worry about the entities *leaving* the small confines of the closet. She had the very distinct impression that they gravitated to that area for some reason and didn't bother with other areas of the house.

Cheryl informed them that they could say prayers and let the entities know that they could freely "leave" this realm if they so desired, but other than that, she could only offer one suggestion to keep the spirits at bay: Get a potted sage plant and place it in the doorway to the linen closet. This would ensure that the negative energy within *stayed* in the small space of the closet. Sage, she informed them, was a mystical plant with cleansing powers that had been used by many cultures throughout the centuries for rituals involving purification and exorcism. Sort of in the way garlic was rumored to ward off vampires, sage, especially when burned as incense, had the power to tame negative forms of energy.

"For some reason I don't get the impression they want to leave that space," she explained. "They're mad about something and don't want to come out. But if they *were* to leave that closet for some reason and enter other areas of your home, it wouldn't be a pretty sight. You'd have a *real* problem on your hands then..." Observing the look of concern on their faces, she added: "Just put a sage plant in the doorway and you'll be fine." Realizing she hadn't quite assuaged their fears, the psychic quickly tried to change the subject from the five malevolent powers upstairs to the two kinder beings on the ground floor. "The old woman and the little girl down here are very happy," she added. "They feel very much at home, and they want you to feel that way, too. The little girl's presence is especially strong."

With a bit of a jolt, Jon suddenly regained his speech and looked at Barb. "Show her the pictures from the New Year's Day parties!" he insisted. Without a word, she ran to a nearby drawer and returned with several stacks of 35mm color prints. As she rummaged through the bundle, Jon repeated the information he had shared earlier about their annual get-together on January 1, pointing out that something strange started to happen after they moved into 539 West Saint Catherine. "Look!" Barb said, handing Cheryl first one stack of photos, then another. "Remember what you said about the little girl liking the fact that she had so many children to play with? Look at these..."

With Jon and Barb looking on, the psychic slowly sifted through both files of prints, a smile forming on her lips as she stared at the last of the pictures. "How *unusual*," she remarked, as she lay the two stacks down and then started to go through the first, and then the second. "As I said, Rose has a very strong presence here, and I think these photos make this quite clear. These pictures are from the first year you had this party in the house?" she inquired, setting the first pile down so she could devote her attention to the second pile in front of her.

"That's the thing," interjected Jon with an energetic nod of the head, "those are from two years in a row now! Every time we have the New Year's Day party here it happens. The first year it happened, we just thought there was something wrong with the film or the camera, but when it happened the second year, we started to wonder. We didn't really put two and two together till you made that comment about Rose liking all the kids in the house." He took a step towards her and started to shift through the photos himself.

One by one, he laid the pictures from the first stack down on the small table in the foyer, spreading them out as he did so. One had a young couple posed in front of a lovely carved wooden mantel draped in garland and ribbon; the next showed a middle-aged man with specs pushed down on his nose as he lifted a cup of holiday punch in a toast; another had several elderly adults sitting around the counter in the kitchen. All in all, nothing out of the ordinary could be seen, just random faces and bodies, groups of coworkers and friends, neighbors and couples, all in festive surroundings.

With the next stack of pictures, he started to sift through and spread them out on the wooden surface in front of them all; however, this was not the case. One by one, he picked out a color print, held it up for examination and then put it down. In each of these, it became obvious that a child or children had been the subject matter for the photographer. In some of them, children could be seen playing together on the throw rug in front of the cozy fireplace in the front parlor, or else darting around among the adults gathered in the kitchen. Some of the other photos showed individual infants, or smiling little boys or girls sitting on a parent's knee, standing next to the Christmas tree, eating a cookie...

Aside from the children present in each of the pictures, they all had something in common: oddities in the photos that appear to be bright flashes of orange light, hazy yellow blurs and streaks of something small that seem to have been moving at speeds too high to be caught on ordinary film. When the two stacks are compared side by side, it becomes obvious that these anomalies can be seen in the pictures of little boys and girls only. In the pictures of the adults alone, not one of these strange manifestations can be observed. Only in cases where adults and children are present in the pictures can you spot these strange occurrences.

Two experts – one a photographic specialist, the other, an old hand in the investigation of psychic phenomena captured on film – have examined the original pictures and negatives from Jon and Barb's holiday parties, and both have come to the same conclusion: They cannot explain what caused the strange appearances in those pictures. Although one or two of the photos with the blinding yellow-orange flashes could technically be attributed to overexposure, the others definitely fall into that small category of rare, unexplained activity that paranormal investigators hope to catch on film when doing research of reputedly haunted houses. Theories abound as to what could possibly account for these odd blurs and streaks of light, but most specialists in the field claim that bona fide psychic events almost always involve a huge output of latent energy, something usually indiscernible to the human eye, yet susceptible to the magnetic properties of ordinary 35mm film.

Jon and Barb don't really care what scientific reasons might explain the weird lights and streaky blurs they caught on film. The strange pictures, coupled with the eerie revelations Cheryl made about the little girl named Rose, seemed to convince them that they live in a haunted house, something they wear as a badge of honor in their neighborhood. As a matter of fact, Barb has confessed that she sometimes feels comforted, sensing that the spirits on the first floor want to protect her. She recalls one snowy evening in winter when quiet sobs and low moans from somewhere in the house caused her to get up and check the house. In the process she startled and scared off a would-be intruder at her back door. "I was frightened at first," she admits, "but when I realized that he might have come into the house if I hadn't gone looking for those strange moans, a sense of calm overcame me, because I had the feeling the old woman was trying to warn me about the danger."

She doesn't have the same positive outlook regarding the five entities in the linen closet on the second floor, however. She took the psychic's advice and placed a potted sage plant on the floor in the doorway of the small room, and since then, she and Jon haven't had any problems with it...or *them.* The animals still seem to be wary of that area, but the sense of uneasiness associated with the closet has noticeably dissipated since Cheryl's visit. Once in a while, both Barb and Jon find themselves staring at the linen closet on the second floor, their uneasy sense of relief tempered with anxiety at the notion of what would happen should their efforts fail to keep the malevolent entities contained in the linen closet. Jon says they enter the small storage room as little as possible and that they make sure the sage is in its spot on the floor at all times. Barb keeps a spare pot in the kitchen, should something happen to the original plant they placed there a year or so ago.

On January 1, 2004, I attended Jon and Barb's annual New Year's Day party at 539 West Saint Catherine. Decorated with garland, colorful ribbons and festive lights, the interior of the house was cozy and inviting, despite the lively throng of guests wandering from room to room. Some nibbled on smoked salmon and cream cheese atop toast points, some demurely sipped champagne, others gulped cups of holiday punch ... most everyone talked about the ghosts and wondered if this year's batch of pictures would produce more of the same strange streaks and blurs as in the previous years. With a 35mm camera around my neck, and a smaller, disposable one at my side, I wandered from room to room as well, snapping pictures between sips of red wine – all the while convinced that I would capture something on film.

While meandering about on the ground floor, I chit-chatted here, stopped for a bit of small talk there, all the while making sure to get shots of adults by themselves, children alone, and adults and kids together. I even devoted an entire roll of 36 exposures to the infamous linen closet on the second floor, mentally provoking the five entities as I boldly crossed the threshold and defied them to manifest themselves. For good measure, I also pounded on the wall and irreverently slammed one of the cupboard doors shut, hoping this might anger them and give them more reason to brood. (And, when no one was looking, I moved the potted herb off to one side and snapped a couple of daring shots *sans* sage.) I couldn't wait to get them developed. I thanked the hosts, finished my glass of wine and ran off to the one-hour photo place.

As is often the case, the one-hour photo service advertised actually turned out to be twenty-seven hour photo service, and I had to wait till the next evening before I could take a gander at the pictures from Jon and Barb's party. One by one, I quickly scanned through each of the photos from the four rolls of film that had been developed. I'm sure the crestfallen look that had overcome me by the time I rifled through the last of the pictures and found absolutely nothing – for the second time – would have been priceless had anyone been present to take my picture, but other than that, it had been a waste of time and money. The party itself was enjoyable, but the pictures were a flop. As consolation, I asked if any of the other photographers present had captured anything, but as far as I know, no one had caught the slightest blur, blip or flash of light. Much to my chagrin, I had scared Rose away.

On a brighter note, I did have a strange occurrence regarding 539 West Saint Catherine several days after that. I had returned during the afternoon hours the next day to get some pictures of the interior of the house and, in addition to some outside shots of Barb and Jon's house, I also took several of the neighboring houses, including one involved in the rumor about the old woman supposedly poisoned by her grandson. Some days later, I had the roll of film developed and found myself at my computer, nonchalantly perusing the pictures, looking for a good exterior shot to go along with this story. I had them placed on a picture disk, and as I viewed the last of them, I was startled to find an old sepia print of a family portrait.

There in front of me, five unknown faces – four male, one female – stared back, their gazes severe and unmoving, as a creepy feeling spread over my body. A woman who could have been anywhere from twenty to forty years old sat on a lone chair with the four men standing behind her, their ages also in the twenty-to-forty-year range, I'd say. From the look of the hairstyles and outfits they wore, it appeared to be in the 1920s or 1930s, but other than that, it was hard to discern anything else concrete about the five somber figures assembled before me. From the dark hair, dark eyes and presumably olive-toned complexions that characterized each of their features, I got the impression that they were of Italian or Greek origin maybe, or definitely something Mediterranean. They had to be related, but I couldn't figure out the actual relationship – perhaps brothers and sister, or cousins? They all had heavy brows and almost brooding dispositions that made me think of the five entities in the linen closet.

Upon closer inspection I could see that the family portrait had frayed edges and a slight crack that wrinkled its way across the surface of the print. It looked like an old picture someone might have had restored, and somehow it ended up on my disk. I called the drug store where I had them developed and asked the manager of the photo desk about this possibility. He said he thought the chances were very slim – albeit not impossible – that something like that could happen. When I sent him a copy of the picture as an email attachment, he commented that he didn't recognize the picture and that, being the manager, he would have seen all restorations in the previous week.

The next strange thing happened when I was sorting through the pictures again, in search of a frontal shot for one of the neighboring houses to 539 West Saint Catherine. As I compared two photos, my eyes were drawn to the shadows in an upper right-hand window, and I realized I could discern several vague forms. Upon closer examination the photo revealed what appeared to be the shadowy figures of a young child leaning forward on the window sill and an old woman in a nightgown standing behind. The child appeared to be dressed in a shirt with a solid stripe across the chest, and the grandmotherly shape seemed to have her hair done up in a bun and had a hand resting on the child's shoulder. On the other shoulder rested another hand, however, from the angle and size, it appeared to belong to another, unseen, figure.

I tried a little experiment and showed that picture, along with several others, to about ten friends and asked if they could pick out anything odd about any of the shots. I made sure not to tell them what to look for, either. All ten were drawn to the photo where I had seen the strange figures in the shadows, and five of them quickly identified a child perched at the window ledge, and then, an older woman standing behind – and all without any prompting. The other five agreed they recognized the shapes after I pointed them out by tracing the edges with the tip of a pencil. For curiosity's sake, I had the picture enlarged, and printed in black and white as well. I was amazed to see that individual fingers and thumbs were clearly visible on each of the hands, something that had gone unnoticed on the smaller prints. When most viewers study the enlargements, they usually point out the shapes of a young child and old woman right away. Whether or not these shapes come as nothing more than the coincidental result of odd shadows and reflections caught in the pane of glass, no one has told me. Nobody has been able to say that they're lost spirits randomly caught on film, either.

In any case, these two events relating to the pictures taken around 539 West Saint Catherine definitely make the story more interesting – not that it needed anymore details to add interest. Barb and Jon have slowly accustomed themselves to the idea of living in a house with disembodied spirits and they claim it doesn't really bother them anymore. Although something strange and unexplained still happens from time to time, like the loud crash of breaking glass or quiet sobs emanating from somewhere in the house, they say the activity died down considerably after their last-minute visit from Cheryl. As time passes, Jon and Barb slowly dig up bits and pieces of the lives lived in 539 West Saint Catherine, but they have yet to uncover anything about a little girl with red hair named Rose, or any concrete details about the old woman whose grandson might have poisoned her, or any reasons why five brooding spirits might have a penchant for the confines of the linen closet on the second floor. Till then, they will wait patiently and see what they can uncover, always making sure the ceramic pot with the live sage plant is in its spot on the floor in front of the linen closet.

Photographic experts cannot explain the strange phenemena on the pictures taken at 539 West St. Catherine.

Photos courtesy of Jon Huffman and Barb Cullen.

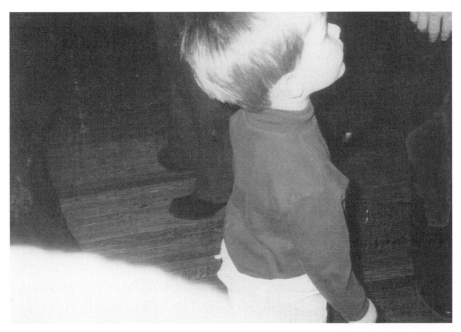

Could the photographic anomalies on these pictures be attributed to the ghost of a young girl who loves to play?

Photos courtesy of Jon Huffman and Barb Cullen.

ABOUT WAVERLY HILLS
TUBERCULOSIS SANATORIUM

Anyone at all familiar with Louisville has heard about the infamous tuberculosis sanatorium at Waverly Hills in the city's south end – and the countless stories of hauntings and strange events surrounding it. A titanic four-story, art-deco masterpiece with more than four hundred rooms at one time, it sits alone and abandoned, looming over Dixie Highway while the ravages of time take their toll. For more than twenty years it has stood empty and waiting while inclement weather destroys the roof and exposes its delicate interior to the elements, while thoughtless vandals and hoodlums add to the damage, and a derelict landlord and a community largely indifferent to its plight sat back and watched it slip further from the grasp of restoration, all seemingly oblivious to the important piece of Louisville history decaying in front of them.

As if living up to its nickname as *The Graveyard of the West,* Louisville by 1900 enjoyed the dubious honor as the city with the highest tuberculosis death rate in the nation. Area infirmaries had a difficult time tending to the high numbers of the sick and dying, and, as a result, officials approved construction of a wooden hospital atop the windy perches of Waverly Hills in 1910 to better provide patients an abundant supply of fresh, clean air. Louisville historian Tom Owen explains, "The preferred treatment in those days included extended bed rest with plenty of fresh air and sunshine, and a long period of convalescence." Originally planned for 40 patients, Waverly Hills usually held at least three times that many, and by the early 1920s it had outgrown its usefulness. Built in 1926, the structure standing today provided some degree of comfort to untold numbers of TB victims till it closed in 1961, when improvements in hygiene and the emergence of antibiotics led to a drastic reduction in the number of TB cases. Most records have been lost, but some local historians estimate the number of total dead to be in the tens of thousands, something almost impossible to substantiate without the proper medical documents. One thing relatively certain, however, is that at the height of the epidemic in the 1920s, an average of one person per hour died at Waverly Hills, their bodies subsequently relegated to an unceremonious disposal through the notorious "body chute."

According to eyewitness accounts, this body chute, or "death tunnel" as it also came to be known, saved the residents from witnessing a steady parade of death out the door. Instead of constantly wheeling the cadavers past the surviving patients, orderlies surreptitiously hauled them through the underground passage to hearses waiting at the bottom of the hill. If so instructed, hospital authorities immediately cremated some of the bodies on the premises. As a result of the untold amount of human death and suffering within the walls of the old sanatorium, a certain mystique about Waverly Hills has arisen that has spawned many legends and tales of hauntings.

Accordingly, the Louisville Ghost Hunter's Society, one of the largest and most prestigious in the nation, has become involved with paranormal research conducted at the ruins of Waverly Hills. If anyone can be considered an authority on the supernatural goings-on at the old sanatorium, its president, Keith Age, and vice president, Jay Gravatte, would fit the bill. Both have spent hours exploring the rambling spaces of the decaying building, collecting data and research for an upcoming book documenting the eerie events they've experienced at Waverly Hills. During a recent interview, Jay Gravatte shared his recollections of one "memorable" evening at the sanatorium while assisting the camera crew for the taping of a well-known reality series.

"My duty that night was simple: Take several girls through Waverly Hills for the Fox reality series, *'Scariest Places on Earth.'* I had to explain some of the history surrounding the abandoned hospital," he recalls, "and recount some of the paranormal activity experienced there." Jay had devised a simple plan: film everything they encountered while taking the women on their tour. The program directors would use whatever footage they found interesting for the show.

He remembers it was an unusually hot July day, when they arrived at Waverly Hills. "I could tell the girls were feeling apprehensive before we had even entered the old hospital. All they could see was this hulk of a building as it sat there like a conquered and battered ruin." At the main entrance, Gravatte told the story of an apparition often sighted in that location – something he described as "a woman running out of the front door, her hands and legs in chains, crying and pleading for help." Taking note of the nervous glances the girls had been exchanging, he also pointed out a third-story window, where a young girl of seven or eight had been seen on occasion. According to Gravatte, "this set the mood for the night to come."

Jay swung open the old doors and led the girls inside. After several moments in the lobby, they entered a room directly adjacent to the main entrance. Originally used as the medical director's office, it would be used as a 'safe room' for the girls." Chairs, food, and water had been set up in the room, in case they needed a break while filming or needed some place to run if things got out of control. Jay then proceeded to take them down to the medical wing on the first floor.

"This involved a trip through the so-called 'death wing' where the morgue and autopsy room had been located," he recalls. Walking down the dingy hallway, they entered the infamous body chute, the converted coal tunnel allegedly used to transport dead bodies from the hospital to the crematorium located down the hill. As they made their way down the tunnel and up toward the second floor, Gravatte then told the girls about *Ralph*, a ghostly maintenance man in white who has been spotted on various occasions. He had been describing the apparition when an eerie red light started to illuminate the entire end of the hallway. "Of course," he explains, "the girls began screaming and nearly ran me and the film crew down trying to get out of there."

After calming them down, he escorted them to the safe room for a break and then continued with the tour. Once they had made the rounds of the other floors, Gravatte says they returned to the first floor and the area around the old morgue. As he stood there, one of the huge wooden doors slammed shut, causing him to jump back in surprise. They had barely regained their composure when something small and metallic could be heard bouncing down the hallway. "It turned out to be an old time bottle cap from a soda," he explains. "Just out of the blue, like that…" Jay says this drove the girls over the edge and sent them back down the hallway for another break in the safe room."

According to Jay, Keith Age then took over, and within moments, "the electromagnetic field meter started clicking and was jumping up the scale." A piece of equipment used in ghost hunting, an electromagnetic field meter, or EMF meter, can detect the disturbances in the natural electromagnetic field produced when "ghosts" or other paranormal phenomena are present. According to Age, the meter should not have gone off in the building unless it encountered something magnetic. "Electricity had been disconnected in the '80s, but strangely enough, the meter continued to react to something – and whatever it was, it was moving."

When they followed the signal to a small room divided in half with a cinderblock wall, "the meter spiked to the top of the scale and squealed like it had never done before." The sound of breaking glass could be heard and the needle froze in place at its highest position. Age claims the EMF reader stopped making the high-pitched noise, but then started to heat up in his hand. "So hot – in fact – that solder actually melted on the circuit board and started to drip out of the meter." Age had pulled the battery out in an attempt to prevent more damage when the group noticed a considerable drop in the room's temperature – from 74 to 52 degrees, despite the hot summer weather outside. When they later consulted the floor plans for the old hospital, they were more than a little surprised to discover that the chamber had been used a an electroshock therapy room at one time.

Age walked down the hall with his group and came to a small room with a heavy metal door and eight poles connected to the ceiling from the floor. From these poles four additional rods ran horizontally and connected to the walls, and a large drain sat on the right side of the floor. For many, this room has become one of the creepiest parts of the Waverly Hills experience. According to rumor, this small chamber served as *the draining room*, a macabre last stop on the road to eternity for many unfortunate tuberculosis victims.

Jay Gravatte says that during the heyday of the tuberculosis hospital, people were dying so quickly that bodies had to be removed from the hill as quickly as possible so as to free up beds for other patients. Residents of Jefferson County supposedly refused to have these infected bodies in their midst, and, since Waverly had no cemetery, officials came up with the best solution they could: The corpses would be hung from the poles in the room and then slit lengthwise to drain them of their bodily fluids. They were then whisked away down the body chute.

On an even more macabre note: Some claim that when tuberculosis became less threatening in the 1930s, hospital staff used the room as a smokehouse to cure the meat from livestock raised and slaughtered on the grounds.

The small group then ascended the stairs to the fifth floor, a part of the old hospital notorious for frequent paranormal activity. Officials reportedly housed mentally insane tuberculosis patients in two locations on this floor, and two rooms, 502 and 506, monitored the ward in 18-hour shifts. According to one story, a head nurse was found dead in room 502 in 1928. She had apparently hanged herself in a fit of depression. The county coroner decided the 29-year-old woman – unmarried and pregnant – had committed suicide.

In 1932, another nurse who worked in room 502 supposedly jumped from a balcony and killed herself as well. Local legends claim she was pushed or driven to suicide by the many tormented souls that still linger among the ruins of Waverly Hills. But that's where the reality and fantasy associated with the old hospital start to merge and become vague. Keith Age recalls that room 502 that night did experience many sudden rises and drops in temperature. Others have reported strange, haunting moans and screams emanating from room 502. Some have seen pallid apparitions of sickly women with haggard faces; a few have even reported sightings of an old-fashioned, horse-drawn hearse noisily bolting down the drive leading from the old sanitarium. These are only a small fraction of the unnerving tales that have become so typical for Waverly Hills. The book Jay Gravatte and Keith Age are working on, with noted paranormal investigator Troy Taylor, will make a fascinating addition to the rich lore and legacy surrounding Waverly Hills, one of the most haunted spots in the entire USA.

Like many landmarks in Louisville – and around the country – the tuberculosis hospital at Waverly Hills has paid the price for a community largely indifferent to the fate of so many of its architectural gems. As if years of neglect weren't bad enough, the previous owner tried to have the sprawling building condemned when he couldn't raise enough money to have the world's tallest statue of Jesus built atop the site. Since the overall solidity and excellent construction of the hospital had preserved the structural integrity of the building, he tried to "help" it along in its demise by digging out large sections of the foundation, among other things...

But, Waverly Hills still stands, keeping silent watch over the south end of Louisville, as the ghosts from its past wander its halls and grounds. A couple recently purchased the imposing fortress and has established a historical society to "preserve" Waverly Hills before she succumbs to the hardships the last twenty years have dealt her. I hope it's not too late.

Several miles away, Old Louisville sits, safely tucked away for the time being, beneath a leafy canopy of green and gold that fades in the fall and disappears all together in the winter. While brick and mortar crumble off the still noble facade of Waverly Hills, Old Louisvillians paint their shutters and prune the azalea bushes in preparation for autumn. When the first parched leaf lets go and silently cascades to the sidewalk below, something unseen in the ground starts to pulsate, and a signal runs quietly through the neighborhood. People feel the vibration in their feet and on the tips of their fingers when they notice the first bristle of chill fall air about them. Somewhere off in the distance, as a milky pall of gray creeps up over the horizon, something clicks and hisses. A tiny spark ignites and flickers, and then mellows into a soft, orange glow as the panes of crystal in the old gas lamps gratefully accept the warmth.

Day is gone.

It is just before dark.

It is the time ghosts start to wander the streets in Old Louisville.

AFTERWORD

When I first mounted the steps leading to 1228 South Third Street, it was the afternoon before Christmas. The house that stood before me sparked a tender feeling in my heart, making me believe that I was entering someplace out of a storybook or fairy tale. This historic Victorian home, painted in a bright red brick color with green and gold leaf trim to highlight exquisite architectural details, shone in the bright winter sunshine as a few snowflakes were falling. Since that first magic encounter, I have experienced many other moments to be cherished in this house called Widmer House – the home of the author of this book, David Dominé.

At David's parties, dinners and smaller gatherings here, I have met many unique and talented people. And I've never felt an awkward moment – only fellow feeling and good cheer. The unique décor, David's fabulous cooking and his charm as a host make this a favorite spot for many. In one of the stories in this book, David has suggested that this house is haunted. This is difficult for me to fathom, since all I have ever experienced here is an incredible hospitality. Could Widmer House really be haunted? And the other Old Louisville sites that he mentions in this book that are also dear to me – could they be haunted, as well? In David's book, the lively scenes, the firsthand reports of those who say they have seen ghosts, and the intricate plots that emerge when spirits become characters have caused me to second-guess my own experience.

And what about other sites in Old Louisville that are not mentioned here? I have been a professor at Spalding University at 851 South Fourth Street for fifteen years. Although not technically within the bounds of Old Louisville, the architectural treasure of this university – the Tompkins-Buchanan-Rankin Mansion – is clearly one of Louisville's rarer gems. This Italianate Renaissance revival home is one of the few remaining structures designed by architect Henry Whitestone; it is a Kentucky Landmark and listed on the National Register of Historic Places. Whitestone completed the mansion in 1871 for a local importer, Joseph T. Tompkins. In 1880, it was purchased by a distiller, George Buchanan. When he went bankrupt in 1884 and put the house up for auction, it was purchased by another distiller, Rhodes B. Rankin. In 1918, this "851 Mansion," as it is also called, was sold to the Sisters of Charity of Nazareth, who opened Nazareth College. This college later became Spalding University. Could this old mansion, at the heart of Spalding University, possibly be haunted or have ghosts?

During the fifteen years that I have been teaching at Spalding, I have been assigned a couple of offices located on the upper floors of this mansion. I will admit that the radiators in these offices have, on occasion, given vent to some eerie moans and groans, but it never crossed my mind that I might be hearing the cries of former residents, such as Buchanan going bankrupt. I have also been a guest at a number of receptions and parties held on the first floor of the mansion where many architectural features of ornate beauty can be seen. At these events, I have often marveled at the etched Viennese glass that make up the door panels, never suspecting that the sound of a light clinking of glass that I have heard from time to time was anything other than the sound of colleagues toasting to something special. I have been up and down the original 1871 hand-carved walnut staircase over one thousand times and the only mysterious thing I have ever noticed was light flickering in from a stained glass skylight onto the intricately carved walnut rosettes, florets and leaves that grace the entire staircase.

But, of course, I have always been somewhat of a skeptic when it comes to ghosts. After reading David's finely crafted and often haunting stories, however, I will definitely pay closer attention to what is happening around me. Marion Wilson, a colleague and friend, recently told me, in fact, that they've heard rumors that Spalding's Center Building is haunted. She explained that "during World War II, the building was used by the USO as a place for soldiers to relax." There are rumors circulating that their partying can still be heard, as well as stranger things." *Hmmmmm.*

I will have to admit, I don't know about that. Sitting here with my cat in my lap, I have to wonder…What I do know is that David's sensitivity to the stories he has heard and to the people he writes about attests to his extraordinary capacity to enter into the inner lives of others. This, to me, is a sign of a gifted writer. His knowledge of the history and architecture of Old Louisville is also remarkable. The moods and pictures he creates with words are haunting, vivid and true, if not enviable. As for the past lives of this, the country's largest Victorian neighborhood, he may very well be *the* expert on the subject. He has saved a bit of the past that might have been lost forever. In this book, the ghosts of Old Louisville creak back to life…moaning, groaning and smiling.

Judy Cato
Louisville, October 31, 2004

ACKNOWLEDGEMENTS

I would like to thank all who helped make this book a reality, including the staff of the Filson Club Historical Society, the Louisville Free Public Library, the Old Louisville Information Center, the Friends of Central Park, the library and archives at the University of Louisville, the Conrad-Caldwell House, the Brennan House, the Louisville Ghost Hunters Society and the Kentucky State History Center in Frankfort. I'd also like to thank Debra Richards of the Louisville Landmarks Commission and Marion Wilson of the Spalding University Library for their research assistance. In addition, I owe a huge debt of gratitude to writers and historians such as Samuel W. Thomas, William Morgan, Wade Hall, George Yater and Melville O Briney who have contributed so much to the recording and documenting of Old Louisville history. Roberta Simpson Brown has been especially inspiring with her many entertaining tales of hauntings and ghosts in this area of the country, and so has Troy Taylor.

For their encouragement and support, thank you to Jon Huffman, Barb Cullen, Rhonda and Michael Williams and the West Saint Catherine Street Neighborhood Association and the 1300 South Third Street Neighborhood Association. I'm particularly grateful to Jay Gravatte, Keith Age, Kelly Atkins and Tom Owen for their expertise and to friends and fellow writers, Jerry Lee Rogers and Judy Cato, for their encouragement and input. To Paula Cunningham, Michelle Stone and the staff at McClanahan Publishing House: Thank you for all your assistance and for taking on this project in the first place.

Above all, thank you to the people of Old Louisville for enthusiastically sharing their stories and tales with me. Thanks to Rocky, Bess and Ramón for putting up with me – and to the members of the Thursday Night Dinner Club, a big *Cheers!*

Many photographs in *GHOSTS OF OLD LOUISVILLE* come courtesy of Anetria Brownlee, a dedicated teacher at Young Elementary School in Louisville, where she teaches Spanish. The Old Louisville resident pursues many interesting pastimes, including frequent visits to Mexican restaurants, but foremost among her passions is professional photography.